W9-BWV-538

# SHAKESPEARE KIDS

# SHAKESPEARE KIDS

## Performing his Plays, Speaking his Words

**Carole Cox**

LIBRARY
FRANKLIN PIERCE UNIVERSITY
RINDGE, NH 03461

**A Teacher Ideas Press Book**

**Libraries Unlimited**
*An Imprint of ABC-CLIO, LLC*

A B C ● C L I O

Santa Barbara, California • Denver, Colorado • Oxford, England

Copyright © 2010 by Carole Cox

All rights reserved. No part of this book may be reproduced in any form or by any electronic or mechanical means, including information storage and retrieval systems, without permission in writing from the publisher, except by a reviewer, who may quote brief passages in a review. An exception is made for individual librarians and educators who may make copies of portions of the scripts for classroom use. Reproducible pages may be copied for classroom and educational programs only. Performances may be videotaped for school or library purposes.

**Library of Congress Cataloging-in-Publication Data**

Cox, Carole, 1943-
  Shakespeare kids : performing his plays, speaking his words / Carole Cox.
      p. cm.
  "A Teacher Ideas Press Book."
  Includes bibliographical references and index.
  ISBN 978-1-59158-838-2 (pbk. : alk. paper) — ISBN 978-1-59158-848-1 (ebook)
  1. Shakespeare, William, 1564-1616—Dramatic production. 2. Shakespeare, William, 1564-1616—Study and teaching (Elementary) 3. Shakespeare, William, 1564-1616—Study and teaching (Secondary) I. Title.
  PR3091.C69 2010
  792.9'5—dc22      2009041731

14 13 12 11 10    1 2 3 4 5

This book is also available on the World Wide Web as an eBook.
Visit www.abc-clio.com for details.

ABC-CLIO, LLC
130 Cremona Drive, P.O. Box 1911
Santa Barbara, California 93116-1911

This book is printed on acid-free paper ∞
Manufactured in the United States of America

*To the many children and young adults who performed Shakespeare's plays in my elementary school classes, or summer, after-school, or enrichment "Shakespeare for Kids" programs, in Madison (1968–1973) and River Falls (1970–1972), Wisconsin; Baton Rouge, Louisiana (1980–1983); and Long Beach (1991–1996) and Los Angeles (1995), California, as well as their families and friends, with my thanks.*

# Contents

# Preface

You will read more about the first time I tried doing Shakespeare with my fourth/fifth-grade class at Shorewood Hills Elementary School in Madison, Wisconsin, in 1968. Fast forward to the Fourth of July weekend of 2005, however, for the real impetus for the book. My former students had been communicating with me and each other over many years about our classes and why they were memorable. They decided to hold a reunion and also invited the many children who had participated in the summer "Shakespeare for Kids" program I created through the parks and recreation department from 1969 to 1973. Although I expected there might be a few people for coffee, there were many, many more, including not only former students but also their parents, families, spouses, and participants in the Shakespeare summer program. And the thing that struck me as I spoke with them over the long weekend during the many wonderful events they planned was how often they wanted to talk about their experiences doing one of Shakespeare's plays with me so many years ago. I began to see that I had to write this book to share with other teachers, librarians, parents, and students how we did it, and to encourage them to try it themselves.

When I thought I had finished the book, I had an odd feeling that something was still missing. I finally realized it was the voices of my students. I had written about my experience of what we did and tried to describe what they might have thought and felt. But why not go to the source? I used the listserv some former Madison students had worked so hard to compile to contact people for the 2005 reunion; added e-mail addresses I had for students in other times and places, including my own three children, Wyatt, Gordon, and Elizabeth; and sent out a request for any memories they would like to share about performing one of Shakespeare's plays with me. You will see what they wrote throughout the book, adding their voices to mine for a more complete picture of the experience for all of us.

I hope you will listen to the enthusiasm and joy in their voices and use this book to have as much fun as I did with all the Shakespeare kids I directed over the years, performing his plays and speaking his words.

# Introduction

## TEACHING SHAKESPEARE THROUGH PERFORMANCE, GRADES 3–8

I'll begin by sharing a story of my own experience as an elementary teacher and the first time I tried performing one of Shakespeare's plays from a script condensed for children. What surprised me was that my students led the way. I had to go through a process of demythologizing my adult view of performing Shakespeare with my young students. In this book I address each of the myths that teachers or other adults might have, based on my experience performing the plays with hundreds of students, grades 3–8, and sometimes even younger students. I also provide an overview of the steps for performing a play in the classroom, library, or Shakespeare-for-children summer, enrichment, or after-school program.

## MY FOURTH/FIFTH-GRADE CLASS AND *HAMLET*

I began to do Shakespeare with children almost by chance. We received a class set of Scholastic's newspaper for children, *Newstime*, every week. I usually just passed it out during the last period of the day, and we would all dive in and start reading, discussing articles of interest before everyone went home. One week *Newstime* included a script of *Hamlet*, condensed from the original by Shakespeare by Albert Cullum, a teacher in Boston. There was a brief introduction about doing the play in the classroom, with an illustration of obviously young actors performing it.

As my students read, it wasn't long before someone raised a hand and asked me innocently, and in front of everyone, if our class could perform the play. Put on the spot, and feeling a bit of panic I didn't quite understand, I had to think fast. And my thoughts were: We can't do *Hamlet*! It's Shakespeare! How can I do Hamlet with children? (I had no idea how to do Shakespeare with adults!). It's too hard! How will they understand it! (I don't think I understand it!) And the most insidious thought of all: What if we fail? I was more concerned about failing and losing face as a teacher in front of other teachers and adults than I was in losing face with my students.

But how could I say no to this student, when I had told the class all year how great they were at drama? We had written and performed play scripts based on literature and folktales related to social studies or just for pleasure. We wrote and performed original scripts for plays, musicals, and movies we made. But still I hesitated, despite the obvious student interest I was sensing in the classroom about doing this play.

Then, like the Grinch, I had what I thought was a wonderful (awful) idea. I asked my students: "Who can explain what the play means?" Never mind that I didn't feel I could explain it; I was the teacher and standing in front of the class. The room became quiet, in part, I think, because that was not the kind of question I tended to ask. They may have been suspicious. By then it was the end of the day, and when the bell rang, I thought I was safe. *Hamlet* would go away. But another student asked if we could talk again the next day about performing *Hamlet*. Still trying to wriggle out of a tight spot, I said, "Well, maybe, if anyone can explain the meaning of the play." I smugly thought I had defused the situation.

The next day proved me wrong. They wanted to talk about *Hamlet*. Some had brought a paperback copy of the play to class. Others had written some notes. I wondered if they had talked to their parents about it. So I had to ask, "Who can explain the meaning of the play *Hamlet*?" Several students shared things that happened in the play. I said, "Yes, but who can explain what it means?" Then Howie tentatively raised his hand. He explained that he thought Hamlet was confused about things he didn't know or understand, like how he felt about Ophelia or how his father had died so suddenly or why his mother had so quickly married his uncle and seemed so happy, even though he thought she had loved his father. I will never forget what he said as he finished: "I think the problem is that Hamlet has a lot of doubts." It was dead silent in the room. All eyes were on me. I knew they knew they had me. Howie had given a good explanation of *Hamlet*, a play we had not studied but had only read about briefly in a student newspaper. How could I say we couldn't try to perform the play? I couldn't.

So we tried *Hamlet*, because I thought we shouldn't fail for lack of trying. I decided I'd rather risk losing face with other teachers and adults than risk losing it with my students. If it meant murdering Shakespeare, so be it. But it worked. We all learn by doing, as I did by teaching Shakespeare through performance to these fourth- and fifth-grade students. And the first thing I learned to do was get past the myths I held about performing his plays with children.

# FIVE MYTHS ABOUT PERFORMING SHAKESPEARE WITH CHILDREN

I learned to demythologize my own adult perceptions of doing Shakespeare with children, which were based on no experience whatsoever. With experience, my students proved me wrong about all of them.

## Myth 1: Children will not understand the language and ideas in Shakespeare's plays

I found that Shakespeare's language and ideas are not too difficult for children to read and comprehend at their developmental level of understanding. No one will ever grasp all of Shakespeare at one time. His plays are too rich a storehouse of human thought and emotion. We can return to him again and again, at different times in our lives and under different circumstances, and still find some new meaning. That is what has made him one of the world's greatest storytellers and why we are still fascinated with his work today, hundreds of years after he told his stories.

## Myth 2: You have to change Shakespeare's language for children

I do not change Shakespeare's language when I condense a play for children, because I have found that they love to roll his words and phrases around on their tongues, savoring the verbal feast and relishing the rhythm of his verse. Shakespeare is a perfect way to develop a child's taste for a gourmet vocabulary. Words or phrases that are new or unusual can be discussed and explained just like vocabulary in every other subject. The more complex academic vocabulary of mathematics, science, and social studies has to be learned by children in school, so why not Shakespeare? Some estimate Shakespeare coined and added 1,700 words to the English language, and some would argue that he invented modern English. It seems to me it is certainly worth the effort to make this a part of the learning experience of any child in an English-speaking classroom.

# Myth 3: Children will not be interested in the plays

I think children are fascinated with the plays because they are fascinating. Shakespeare's plots, settings, characters, and language cover the depth and breadth of human, and some inhuman, experience and emotion and can surprise and enlighten and delight children even as they do adults. There are comedies and tragedies and romances, adventure and history and mysteries. There are stories of conflict and war, love and hate, envy and admiration, revenge and redemption, good versus evil, magic and reason, clowns and buffoons, causes and cowards, doubt and deception These are the same things that children find interesting in the books they read or movies they watch or video games they play.

# Myth 4: It is too difficult for children to memorize lines, develop characterizations, or handle staging

Children work hard at memorizing lines, developing characterizations, and handling staging, just as they would if they were performing any other type of play and just as older students or adults would do when they perform a play. I condense the plays for children to play about 30–45 minutes, and the lines are manageable. Children are highly motivated to learn the lines, and they are meaningful because they are acting them out and want to do their best when performing. It takes some time and lots of practice, but that is true of anything they learn to do well, and that is worth doing.

I don't remember Shakespeare ever being difficult to understand. I had just turned seven when I performed my first Shakespeare play, and learning the script and the story was no different from mastering any other book I studied in school or at home. As a young child just learning to read, every piece of literature was new to me. What difference did it make if it was Dr. Seuss or Shel Silverstein or William Shakespeare? If I didn't know what a word meant, I asked. That is how one learns.

As far as memorizing? Never underestimate the capacity of a child to memorize lines. By that age, I could recite several Disney movies line-for-line. And though for the plays I performed, I needed only to memorize my own part, I distinctly remember each cast member knowing at least the lines of every character with whom we had a scene, if not most of the lines from the whole play.

Understanding the concepts of the plays was no different. Shakespeare's works contain allegories and archetypes that are present elsewhere in a child's literary world: comedy and tragedy; kings and queens; witches and fairies; tales of revenge and love. These themes are universal across centuries, across lands, and across generations.

Elizabeth Spates, in Carole Cox's "Shakespeare for Kids" summer program,
Long Beach, California, 1991, 1992, 1993, 1994, 1995, and 1996

## Myth 5: The plays could not be performed well enough to interest an audience

An audience composed of parents is perhaps not a good measure of audience interest, but I have never done the plays with just parents for an audience. We always had other family, friends, and members of the community at our plays. Newspaper and television reporters were always very interested in what we were doing.

In Madison, Wisconsin, where I did six plays each summer in the city recreation program, the plays received serious reviews in the theater section of the local paper. In Baton Rouge, Louisiana, our plays were a fixture on television news shows and drew crowds of a few hundred. In Long Beach and Los Angeles, California, we performed *Macbeth* as part of the Shakespeare Festival/LA after a docent saw some of my children spontaneously acting out scenes from Shakespeare while visiting the Shakespeare Family Festival that preceded the performance and asked, "Who are these kids?" People may have come initially because they were curious, but I think they came back because it was entertaining. One fan told me: "Carole, I like the way you do Shakespeare best. It's fast-paced, fun, and it's short."

**Banquo, Macbeth, and the three witches in *Macbeth*, at the
Shakespeare Festival/LA**

I remember performing in *Hamlet* and *Macbeth* vividly. To me, it seemed easy and normal at the time to be doing Shakespeare in fourth and fifth grades. My roles were a soldier in *Hamlet* and Lady Macbeth. I remember how amazed my mother and her friends at the university were that a class of fourth and fifth graders were performing Shakespeare, but at the time I don't remember it being any more challenging than the other plays we did. I remember such a feeling of pride when my mother would tell her friends the plays we were doing, and they would be astonished, and ask me what role I played. I know we had a condensed script that was meant to be easier for young people to perform, but not much was lost as far as the story and themes. I loved the costumes, the language, and the feeling of doing Shakespeare. Later in life, when the lines from the play would come to me I would think back to the memories of doing the play with Mrs. Cox, and always felt like those were "my" plays. I would hear a line or a reference to *Hamlet* or *Macbeth* and think "Oh we did that play when I was in elementary school." Or I would see a famous actress playing Lady Macbeth and think "That was my role!" Doing Shakespeare's plays in Mrs. Cox's class was something that stayed with me for my life. It gave us all great confidence and was a wonderful life experience.

Deanna Clark Smith, in Carole Cox's fourth/fifth-grade class,
Shorewood Hills Elementary, Madison, Wisconsin, 1968–1969

One summer I taught a language arts methods class at California State University, Long Beach. On alternate days with the university class I did *A Midsummer Night's Dream* with seven- to eleven-year-olds. I scheduled my university class so that they could attend a dress rehearsal. The college students were a wonderful audience and told the children how much they enjoyed the performance. I told the college students they could ask the children questions. The questions are good examples of the myths held by adults about children performing Shakespeare. The answers are good examples of what children really think and experience.

**Adult:** How did you remember your lines? Was it hard?

**Child:** No, it was very easy. Because we knew what we were saying, what it meant.

**Adult:** How did you stay so quiet backstage?

**Child:** Paying attention to lines and cues meant you had to listen.

**Adult:** How did you feel about playing a boy when you're a girl?

**Child:** As long as it's acting, it's fun.

**Adult:** How did you feel in the love scenes?

**Child:** It's OK if it's not true.

**Adult:** Do you think you or your parents were more involved?

**Child:** My parents didn't do anything. I did it. It was fun.

**Puck eavesdrops on Bottom and Flute practicing the play *Pyramus and Thisbe*, before he turns Bottom into an ass, in *A Midsummer Night's Dream***

My experience has been that children understand a great deal of Shakespeare, as evidenced by their ability to perform his plays with great feeling, style, and energy. If children did not understand the language and ideas, they could not interpret and perform them. I can think of no way to make elementary or middle school children read, memorize, characterize, rehearse, produce, and perform Shakespeare without understanding what they are doing and wanting to do it. I have never done anything with children as a teacher that engaged them and seemed to give them as much joy as performing Shakespeare. Or as one child put it, "This is the funnest thing I've ever done. This guy writes really good stories." Another child, a veteran of one of my summer programs and was waiting to hear what new play we would do that summer, said, "I can't stand the waiting! This is better than Christmas!" It was also the "funnest thing" I had ever done as a teacher.

Two memories keep coming up about my Shakespeare experiences. Both involve you laughing out loud, but not because you were laughing at me, but out of what seemed to be joy at what was happening. The first was in the fourth grade when I turned up for rehearsal, playing the ghost of Hamlet's father, wearing a black robe of some kind and red socks. The red socks seemed to strike you as hilarious. The second was a rehearsal of *Romeo and Juliet* in your summer program and I did Mercutio's death scene, which I recall I did rather dramatically! Much stumbling and falling, all the while facing the audience. In both instances, you laughed out loud with what appeared to be pleasure at the goings on.

Martha Askins, in Carole Cox's fourth/fifth-grade class,
Shorewood Hills Elementary School, Madison, Wisconsin, 1968–1969.

The students in that first class that did *Hamlet*, and hundreds of other children who have performed Shakespeare in my classes, convinced me that having a class perform these plays provides a way to actively engage them with great literature; to develop confidence, self-awareness, and the ability to think on their feet; to work cooperatively with other children; and to gain a strong sense of responsibility to others. The possibilities for language and literacy growth and development are endless. Children learn things from performing Shakespeare that I don't think are possible in any other way: the beauty of his language, his way with words, his timeless stories, and his understanding of the human condition. A teacher performing one of his plays in the classroom could touch the hearts and minds of students forever.

In fourth grade I was in *Hamlet* as Polonius, which has given me a great interest in watching all versions of *Hamlet* and especially focusing on Polonius. . . . Overall, the experiences definitely got me into and interested in theater—and this persists to this day (40 years later!)—it also helps me as a teacher, reminding me that people of all ages learn best by doing—and that sometimes, asking students to dramatize (or turn into comedy) something that we've learned is the best way to sum up our semester.

Felicia Roberts, in Carole Cox's fourth/fifth grade class,
Shorewood Hills Elementary, Madison, Wisconsin, 1968–1969

# OVERVIEW OF THE BOOK

This book is intended to provide teachers of students in grades 3–8, librarians, or adults leading recreational programs with a step-by-step guide for performing one of Shakespeare's plays condensed for children. The book is based on my own experience as a teacher in the elementary classroom and in summer, enrichment, and after-school Shakespeare programs I created. The children I worked with were not selected to be in my class or program. My approach is based on the fact that I taught children across a range of ages and abilities, and I will explain how to differentiate the experience for all students.

There are key ideas in my approach: I condense the plays but never change Shakespeare's language, it is for all children in classes or groups of various sizes, the focus should always be on the children, and I keep it simple.

The rest of the book will take you through this approach step-by-step:

❖ Chapter 1, "Language, Literacy, and Shakespeare for Children," describes a standards-based context and reading research rationale for learning language and literacy by teaching Shakespeare through performance with students in grades 3–8.

❖ Chapter 2, "Choosing a Play," describes how to choose one of ten plays I have done with groups of children, including cross-age groups with children as young as four and five years of age.

❖ Chapter 3, "Condensing a Play," explains how to condense a script to run 30–45 minutes without changing Shakespeare's language

❖ Chapter 4, "Casting a Play," describes my method of letting children cast themselves.

❖ Chapter 5, "Rehearsing a Play," includes simple, practical ideas for staging and rehearsing a play in the classroom, a multipurpose room, or outdoors (I never use stages), including learning lines, blocking the action, and scheduling.

❖ Chapter 6, "Producing a Play," includes simple, practical ideas for producing a play, with ideas for simple costumes and props that children can plan, find, or make, and ways to find and use stage weapons

❖ Chapter 7, "Performing a Play," describes ways to perform the play—always keeping the focus on children—as well as creating programs and doing publicity, planning a pre-performance Renaissance Fair, and using community resources and support.

❖ Appendix A, "Resources for Students and Teachers," includes a selectively annotated list of books to include in a Shakespeare classroom library, as well as Web sites rich with summaries and complete texts of the plays, information about Shakespeare, his work, and his world, and links to many other Web sites and information sources. Books on teaching Shakespeare are included as well as a one-page memo and bibliography to send home to parents so they may explore more books and Web sites with their children.

❖ Appendix B, "*Macbeth* Condensed for Children," is a script that I have used many times with students, beginning in the third grade. I have also revised it for older students and other groups, but it is the script I have used the most over time and with many different groups of children. I hope you can use it yourself and introduce children to the magic of the language and stories of the world's greatest storyteller.

# CHAPTER 1

# Language, Literacy, and Shakespeare for Children

This chapter provides a context and rationale for performing Shakespeare with children, showing the relationship among developing age-appropriate language, literacy, and literary understanding in a standards-based environment. This teaching approach is supported by the evidence of current research in reading and language arts. The chapter contains answers to an important question teachers may ask: "In this day of standards, drills, and tests, do teachers still have time for something 'extracurricular,' like performing Shakespeare?"

## MRS. COX, DOESN'T HE KNOW WHO SHAKESPEARE IS?

Students in my third/fourth grade combination class at Shorewood Hills Elementary school in Madison, Wisconsin, were rehearsing *Julius Caesar*. Mark Antony, played by an impassioned Carolyn, had just delivered the famous "Friends, Romans, countrymen, lend me your ears;" soliloquy over the still-twitching body of Caesar, played by a wiggly Eric (we finally covered him entirely with a sheet to help hide the twitches). Carolyn/Mark Antony exhorted the Roman mob to seek vengeance on Eric/Caesar's assassins.

Jeff was the leader of the Roman mob, a part he was born to play. He was a wonderfully intense, animated child who never stopped moving and often struggled to stay focused on school tasks. I usually kept Jeff right next to me in small groups, but he would more often be looking brightly at my face than at his book or paper during a lesson. But Jeff threw every bit of his energy and attention into leading his mob of Roman rabble.

And as he led them out of the classroom and into the hall, wrapped in a Roman toga towel and waving a torch made of a flashlight with the bulb covered with red cellophane, while they yelled "Revenge! Burn! Fire! Kill! Slay!" he encountered the new principal leading a group of university students to observe in my room unannounced. The principal had not expected to find a Roman mob streaming out of my room and said somewhat nervously, "Now, Mrs. Cox does Shakespeare with her students, but I guess we have to decide if this is really part of the language arts program." Jeff, torch above his head and inches from the principal, heard him, turned and looked for me bringing up the rear of the mob, and asked incredulously, "Mrs. Cox, doesn't he know who Shakespeare is?"

1

I remember memorizing the lines "Et tu, Brute? Then fall Caesar!" and lying under a sheet motionless for the remainder of the play. Those words have come back to mind whenever others have tried to "stab me in the back" in the workplace through the years.

Eric Westman, in Carole Cox's third/fourth-grade class,
Shorewood Hills Elementary, Madison, Wisconsin, 1969–1970

My students had learned that Shakespeare was a famous English poet and playwright who lived hundreds of years ago, that his plays were still performed all over the world, and that he was a masterful writer and one of the world's greatest storytellers. Jeff's question was sincere. If Shakespeare was all those things, how could performing his plays not be part of the language arts program?

The principal was simply expressing the mythology I have found surrounding teaching Shakespeare through performance in elementary and middle school: that it would be an extra rather than a basic part of language arts instruction, and questioning if students would be capable of performing or understanding Shakespeare. Jeff was simply expressing how well he understood how Shakespeare could indeed be part of language arts instruction.

I have found this to be true with many other classes and hundreds of students in plays I have produced with them. Shakespeare became a core around which I planned many language and literacy, as well as cross-curricular, activities, which were aligned with curriculum standards and other district and assessment expectations. I describe many more ideas for teaching with drama and integrating the arts across a standards-based curriculum in my textbook, *Teaching Language Arts: A Student-Centered Classroom* (Cox 2008).

I always knew our third/fourth-grade class experience with you in Madison was unique and special. When each of my three children became third graders, your ears must have been ringing as I mentioned to the other parents about how we read and performed Shakespeare's *Julius Caesar*; candid camera should have been there to capture the curious mixture of awe and pain on the parents' faces.

My memory of Shakespeare was that we had FUN getting dressed up and acting. We took the time to understand each character's personality and what made them tick, whether it was Julius Caesar or a plebe. We read our designated character's parts line by line, understood the character's relationships with one another within the context of the scene and the act as the plot unfolded. Though I did not know it at the time, we were empowered by learning to take small steps. It is a lesson I have carried with me ever since. It is a process I have thought and rethought as I prepared for a piano competition in high school, trained and ran the NYC marathon in 2006, or embarked on my job search after opting out for over 10 years to raise a family—three potentially overwhelming projects which were rewarding experiences thanks to the approach of dissecting each project into small pieces and assembling each piece one step at a time. I will always have plenty of projects and challenges. Regardless of their outcome, I will at least have enjoyed and appreciated the process.

Mariko Sakita, in Carole Cox's third/fourth-grade class, Shorewood Hills
Elementary, Madison, Wisconsin, 1969–1970

My first experience with Shakespeare as a grade school student was in third grade. That year, I was put in Mrs. Cox's split-level class with very bright and talented fourth graders. Going into that year, I remember being somewhat intimidated, but also challenged, to be in a class with the older students. The Shakespeare experience was one of many group projects that brought students together and broke down the divisions between the older and younger students.

That year we performed *Julius Caesar*, which is a definite step up from the kind of plays that I assume that we were typically doing in grade school. I say, "I assume," because I have no memory of doing any other plays in grade school. I do, however, remember *Julius Caesar* vividly.

Of course, our collective favorite moment was the assassination scene. With lights flashing, I took my turn to stab the fourth grader, who we all looked up to not only as emperor, but as a class leader. The *Julius Caesar* experience gave us extra confidence in that we felt like we were doing something that was really extraordinary in performing Shakespeare.

The thrill of this collective activity led many of us to eagerly enlist when the Shakespeare experience was extended to a summer theater program by Mrs. Cox, where our classroom stage was replaced by a beautiful setting among the trees on school grounds. No longer tethered to the classroom, we felt even more special as a band of dramatic players. My confidence soared as I was promoted from co-conspirator to a lead role in *A Midsummer Night's Dream*. It felt great to be a lead in this cast of talented children.

In the ensuing summers, we did both *Macbeth* and *Hamlet*. I remember how proud I was to take the stage in the elaborate a costume that my mother had sewn for me. In both these productions, I was cast to share the title role with another boy, who I quickly realized was both far more talented and more precocious than I was. This led me to the humbling recognition that no matter what endeavor you take on, there will always be someone whose star shines brighter and you just have to deal with it. I stayed in touch with this boy for many years afterward, but sadly, he died far too young, in part because of the burdens of harnessing his extreme intellectual gifts.

From the thrills that we got from firsthand experiences with the battle and balcony scenes, and yes, the love and death scenes, those of us who participated in these dramatic experiences at such an early age, not only developed a fondness for Shakespeare specifically, but literature and drama generally. They stand out as three-dimensional representations of the joy of learning and are among my most salient memories from my grade school education. These experiences provided reference points that have come into play throughout my life. And most certainly, they sewed the seeds of confidence for public presentations, which serves me well now as a university professor.

Doug McLeod, in Carole Cox's third/fourth-grade class, Shorewood Hills Elementary, Madison, Wisconsin, 1969–1970, and "Shakespeare for Kids" summer program, 1971, 1972, 1973, and 1974

# LANGUAGE ARTS AND READING THROUGH PERFORMING SHAKESPEARE

Drama and reading are language arts and communication skills that can be integrated in many ways: engagement and motivation, vocabulary growth, comprehension and critical reading skills, extending reading, reading as a thinking process, and creative reading. And what better way to develop language and reading for purpose and meaning might a child have than to understand the written words he or she will speak, interpret, and embody during the performance of a play?

The blocking and staging of the play relies heavily on the skill of ordering, understanding the sequence of events and action, and reacting to it by responding to cues and moving the play forward. In essence, children need to understand the outline of the plot and have a firm grasp of the narrative flow in order to rehearse successfully. Through drama, children are also identifying with the characters they are playing and evaluating character traits, both of which are critical reading skills.

They must also use critical reading skills as they develop their own characters in a play. They must understand the relationship of their characters to other characters and recognize emotional and motivational reactions. What better reading material could be found to teach these two skills than scenes like Lady Macbeth urging Macbeth to murder his king, or Mark Antony's funeral oration over Julius Caesar's body? Scenes from the enchanted world of *A Midsummer Night's Dream* provide ideal reading material to encourage the development of imagination, forming sensory impressions, and reacting to mood or tone in literature.

**Bottom develops his character and makes his fake death funny,
in *A Midsummer Night's Dream***

The creation of costumes, sets, and props requires that children read and research to obtain ideas from many sources. Children are highly motivated to do extensive reading with attention to meaning when the information they are seeking will help them create a Renaissance ball gown for Juliet or her mother, or learn how to use a rapier for Tybalt or Mercutio in a sword fight in *Romeo and Juliet*. During this research, students glean ideas from a great range of sources and thereby extend their reading beyond the play's script.

Children working together to reach the goal of performing Shakespeare must communicate effectively. Throughout the preparation of the play, the activity, language, and ideas of a child form a close relationship. The link between oral and written language and a child's own experience can be strengthened tremendously and must certainly lead to an understanding that reading, especially reading a Shakespeare script, is talking written down, talking that expresses the whole range of human thought, feeling, and emotion. Performing Shakespeare with children can be central, rather than peripheral, to teaching language arts, reading, and literary interpretation in today's standards- and research-based school environments.

Your class had a life-long impact on me. Reading and performing Shakespeare with you in fourth grade was my introduction to the notion of interpretation, to know that there is more than one way to understand a text, that a book can be read for more than plot and character if we only took the time to work at understanding, to learn that something that is opaque on first reading can become more transparent with subsequent readings. It also affected my expectations for my own children's education. Because I was comfortable with Shakespeare as a child, I assumed my own children would be too, and as children so often do, they rose to meet expectations.

Sarah Kianovsky, in Carole Cox's third/fourth-grade class at Shorewood Hills Elementary,
Madison, Wisconsin, 1969–1970

# Standards and Shakespeare

Performing Shakespeare with children can be aligned with national standards in the English language arts and reading.

## *National Standards*

Consider the 12 national *Standards for the English Language Arts* (IRA and NCTE 1996), written jointly by the International Reading Association and the National Council of Teachers of English. The approach described in this book addresses several of them, but most notably the following:

1.  Students read a wide range of print and non-print texts to build an understanding of texts, of themselves, and of the cultures of the United States and the world; to acquire new information; to respond to the needs and demands of society and the workplace; and for personal fulfillment. Among these texts are fiction and nonfiction, classic and contemporary works.

2. Students read a wide range of literature from many periods and many genres to build an understanding of the many dimensions (e.g., philosophical, ethical, aesthetic) of human experience.

3. Students apply a wide range of strategies to comprehend, interpret, evaluate, and appreciate texts. They draw on their prior experience, their interactions with other readers and writers, their knowledge of word meaning and other texts, their word identification strategies, and their understanding of textual features (e.g., sound-letter correspondence, sentence structure, context, graphics).

It should be obvious how performing Shakespeare would address standards 1 and 2 with regard to reading the plays as core works of world literature that add much to our understanding of the human experience, but this experience also clearly addresses standard 3, student learning of word meaning and understanding of texts. One of the most powerful things I learned as a teacher leading students through a production of *Hamlet* was how much my students learned about words while reading a text for understanding, repeatedly reading and then speaking the words aloud and discussing their meaning with each other and me, and then literally acting on the words. Because we were doing a play, their engagement was intense. And because the play might be *Hamlet*, the possibilities for understanding not only words, but ideas and literature, not to mention human nature and history, were limitless.

As I reflect on the experience of doing Shakespeare in your class, I think it might have been the first time I was conscious of the human capacity for critical thinking, or analysis. Not that I would have understood critical thinking as such at that age. And if I wasn't conscious of this capacity, I may have been aware enough of it in some subconscious way to be able to recover it now. But in committing my part of the scripts to memory, I recall wanting to memorize not just the words but the sense and feel of those words, and to absorb the meaning of those words in the context of the narrative. I was conscious that the memorization was made easier by the rhythm of iambic pentameter.

It's more than a little stunning to look back and realize that in the late 1960s, at a time when assassins were gunning down the Rev. Martin Luther King Jr. and Bobby Kennedy, and a nation's hopes and dreams, and at a time when the war in Vietnam was raging and there were both violent and peaceful protests in the streets, we were performing tragedies like *Hamlet* and *Macbeth*—tragedies that were echoing in our contemporary lives and times.

David Medaris, in Carole Cox's fourth/fifth-grade class, Shorewood Hills Elementary, Madison, Wisconsin, 1967–1968 and 1968–1969, and "Shakespeare for Kids" summer program, 1971, 1972, and 1973

# Reading research and Shakespeare

The five "pillars" of reading instruction, which emerged from the *Report of the National Reading Panel* (NICHD 2000), have also been widely used to guide instructional programs and textbook publishing. Performing Shakespeare addresses three of the five in particular: fluency, word meaning/vocabulary, and comprehension.

## *Fluency*

Fluency has recently received increased recognition, and National Reading Panel (NRP) findings established a need for changes in instructional practices. Guided repeated oral reading that included guidance from teachers or peers was identified as one of the practices that had a significant and positive impact on word recognition, fluency, and comprehension across a range of grade levels, and for good readers as well as those experiencing difficulty. Recommended instructional practices include reading aloud, repeated reading, and performance reading. Readers theatre is often suggested as a form of performance reading to develop fluency. Repeated reading aloud of Shakespeare from a script is yet another means to do performance reading.

## *Word Meaning and Vocabulary Instruction*

Word meaning and vocabulary instruction require repeated exposure to words and should be taught both directly and indirectly, with multiple methods rather than relying on a single method. The NRP identifies five instructional methods, all of which can be used while teaching Shakespeare through performance: explicit instruction (e.g., definitions or attributes learned), implicit instruction (e.g., exposure to words), multimedia methods (e.g., going beyond text), capacity methods (e.g., practice), and association methods (e.g., drawing connections with what they already know). Repetition, richness of text, and multiple exposures to words are important, as well as learning in rich contexts that actively engage students, such as rehearsing a scene from Shakespeare.

## *Comprehension*

Comprehension is defined by the NRP as an active process that requires an intentional and thoughtful interaction between the reader and the text. Also valuable for students are problem solving and the ability to relate ideas in print to their own knowledge and experience and construct mental representations in memory. This is exactly what they are doing as they are acting out the ideas and feelings of a scene from Shakespeare.

I have used the types of effective comprehension instruction identified by the NRP when performing Shakespeare with children in the context of reading, analyzing, discussing, rehearsing, and preparing a performance: comprehension monitoring, cooperative learning, use of graphic organizers, question answering, question generation, story structure, and summarization. All these instructional strategies are absolutely essential when teaching Shakespeare through performance. The NRP findings suggest that teaching a combination of these techniques is the most effective and can improve results on standardized comprehension tests. Furthermore, the report suggests that teaching comprehension is also most effective when students are actively engaged, as they would be in preparing to perform a play by Shakespeare.

Finally, Shakespeare's work is core knowledge, his vocabulary rich, his ideas about understanding human experience profound. This is the kind of fundamental knowledge and experience that students gain doing Shakespeare, and it can be clearly related to standards and research, which suggests that a wide academic vocabulary and basic knowledge positively affect performance on standardized tests.

# SHAKESPEARE FOR ALL STUDENTS

People would often comment to me that my Shakespeare classes would be great for gifted students, and of course they were, but that they would be too challenging for students who were not gifted or talented. If they had seen a play, my response was usually to tell them about a child or several children in the production they had seen who had not been identified as gifted, but in fact had another designation, such as "beginning English learner," having a language or a learning disability, "struggling or nonreader," hearing or visually impaired, or behaviorally challenged. This was easy, because every class I taught was inclusive, not exclusive to good readers or gifted and talented and well-behaved students. Shakespeare is for all students.

Shakespeare for Kids has been such a positive factor in the lives of my four children. You seem to be able to offer each child exactly what he or she needs. Here is a parent's view of why this program works:

1. Each child is made to feel special and capable.

2. Ideas contributed by the children are valued.

3. The relationship between the children and the teacher is very open.

4. It is fun!

5. There is an opportunity to interact with a differentiated group of students.

6. The live audience is an exciting reward.

7. It is most challenging.

8. It is enjoyable to work together with a group of friends toward a common goal.

9. Each child experiences success and growth within himself or herself.

A parent of four children of various ages and with very different abilities, in Carole Cox's "Shakespeare for Kids" summer program, Baton Rouge, Louisiana, 1981, 1982, and 1983

There are many ways that performing Shakespeare can be differentiated and meet the needs of all students, and I have had all types of students in my classes. Following are some ideas and examples of real children.

## English learners

I see no reason to limit plays to children who are either native English speakers or English learners at an advanced level of English proficiency. It's important to note that not all English learners in a class or a group will be at the same level of English proficiency, no matter what the grade level. Some may have entered kindergarten not speaking English, but by third grade they will be at an advanced level of oral fluency as well as reading and writing. Others in the same third-grade class may be newcomers and at the very beginning level of learning English, perhaps at the stage of active listening, when they can understand some English but not speak it themselves.

I had two such children in a summer Shakespeare class of *Romeo and Juliet.* They had both just completed third grade in the class of a friend of mine, now a colleague at California State University, Long Beach, Paul Boyd-Batstone. Paul told me they both loved drama. There were both at very different levels of English proficiency, however. Carmen was mature, confident, and fairly fluent in English. She volunteered to be the Duke of Verona and played it with flair. Her strong voice and presence, plus her Spanish accent, brought the Duke to life. Rosalinde, on the other hand, was smaller, very active, and just beginning to speak English. She played a servant of the Montagues, Romeo's family, who argues with a servant of the Capulets, Juliet's family, in the first scene. She also appeared in the ball scene. Carmen helped explain the scene to her in Spanish, and I stood behind her and fed her lines at the beginning, which she learned quickly by first mimicking and then memorizing what I told her. The first time she said them perfectly, I whispered, "Perfect!" in her ear, and we all cheered. Rosalinde, accustomed to repeating what I said, shouted out "Perfect!" as well. She laughed when Carmen explained to her what had happened, but we left the line in the play as a testament to her success. Her physical acting and swagger as the saucy young servant were perfect as well.

Consider how these two English learners and others can experience listening, speaking, and understanding literature in English through drama:

❖ English learners can rely on actions, sound effects, and visual cues such as gestures to both understand and participate in drama.

❖ All students must tap into prior experience, knowledge, and cultural experiences during drama, which is an especially important strategy to use for English learners.

❖ English learners can interact meaningfully with more proficient English learners or native English speakers during drama.

❖ English learners can have partner or buddy roles with a more proficient speaker, such as one of the three witches in *Macbeth*, one of the four fairies in *A Midsummer Night's Dream*, or one of the conspirators in *Julius Caesar*. They can practice scenes together in a small group and support each other during rehearsals.

❖ Teachers can use visual representations of ideas during drama, such as graphic organizers—maps of entrances, actions, and exits—during scene rehearsals.

❖ Creating costumes and props and using music and dance also provide opportunities for English learners to participate fully in drama.

For more ideas on using the arts and literature to teach English learners, see the book I wrote with Paul Boyd-Batstone, the teacher who brought Carmen and Rosalinde to my "Shakespeare for Kids" summer program in Long Beach, California, *Engaging English Learners* (Cox and Boyd-Batstone 2009).

## Students with disabilities

I have had many students with disabilities in my Shakespeare classes over the years. I once had a child who played a terrific Petruchio in *The Taming of the Shrew.* He had a learning disability, was struggling in school with reading, and was very discouraged about reading and school in general. His mother told me that his third-grade teacher had suggested my summer Shakespeare program as a way to engage him with literature and play an active role. His mother told me it would be all right if he didn't have a speaking part. I told her all the children had speaking parts, but we would work together to help him. Doug evidently didn't get the memo about the problems he might have with a speaking part, and volunteered to play the male lead, Petruchio, in *The Taming of the Shrew.* Because I let the students cast themselves, and he was the only volunteer, the role was his. He just looked like a Petruchio—everything about him was funny and slightly crooked, from his T-shirt hanging off one shoulder, to his untied shoes, his uneven curly hair, and even his lopsided smile. I trimmed his lines and encouraged him to play up his ability at physical comedy. His mother taught him his lines orally, and he memorized them. He was a smash. He returned the next summer, and his mother said his reading had greatly improved in fourth grade. He told her he wanted to learn his own lines for Shakespeare the next summer. He played Malcolm, the son of King Duncan, in *Macbeth*, and proudly showed me how he could read those lines.

In a summer production involving fifth- to sixth-grade students, a beautiful and very graceful girl volunteered to play Gertrude, Hamlet's mother. The part was hers. It was only after casting that we learned she was hearing impaired and used a hearing device. I honestly hadn't noticed, and we had only begun to rehearse. She told us she was also a dancer in a junior ballet company. Her parents obviously saw no reason to limit her experiences, nor did I. She learned her lines quickly and spoke them beautifully, and I marveled at how she used visual cues to play her part. She was very disciplined and was my de facto assistant, keeping the more unruly boys in the group in line. Her performance was mesmerizing and regal. I believe she influenced other students' attitudes toward a student with a disability, a positive by-product of trusting students to cast themselves, participate in a heterogeneous group, and not be limited by the expectations of others.

I have very vivid memories of participating in Shakespeare for Kids. I remember when Queen Gertrude introduced herself to the group after the play was cast and explained her hearing deficiency. That took a level of maturity that many people don't have at twice her age.

Scott Ryder, in Carole Cox's "Shakespeare for Kids" summer program in
Baton Rouge, Louisiana, 1980, 1981, 1982, and 1983

Differentiating instruction for students with disabilities will depend on the student and the disability:

❖ The beauty of doing Shakespeare is that all students have an active speaking part, and since you have already condensed the script, you can change, add, delete, or modify it any way you want to accommodate a student.

❖ Every child is involved in performing a play by Shakespeare, which is a key to an inclusive classroom and success for all students.

❖ Students with different disabilities can use different modes to play a part: more physical gestures and actions if reading, speaking, hearing, or language is an issue, or pantomiming actions; using less movement if a child is orthopedically handicapped or movement is otherwise restricted; playing a role with a partner in that role if visually impaired.

❖ Students with disabilities work closely with their nondisabled peers, for an inclusive learning environment.

# Cooperative learning

Cooperative learning strategies support inclusion of all students in a classroom or group and can be used to differentiate instruction for all students when performing Shakespeare. Differences among students, such as cognitive and learning styles, social class, race and ethnicity, language, learning English as a second language, and disabilities, can be viewed as resources. Inclusion is rooted in frequent student-to-student interaction in which students learn about each other as individuals, respect each other, and depend on each other as contributing members of the group. English learners, students with disabilities, struggling readers, or students who are behaviorally challenged may experience success through cooperative learning in these ways:

❖ Filling a group role suited to their strengths or based on their needs.

❖ Listening to scripts read aloud by other students or adults.

❖ Gaining independence through their contribution to group work.

Think of your class or group of students as the characters in one of Shakespeare's plays. Not everyone recites long soliloquies. There are parts of all sizes and types. Some students need to be able to dance or sing or play a clown. Some need to be an intense conspirator or a wretched villain. Some will make you laugh or cry or make you think. There really isn't just one type of part, nor are there any bad parts. There's a good part for every child, and every child can be good in it.

One of the things I remember most about performing Shakespeare in your class and summer programs was a sense of trust. A sense that you trusted our abilities. Trusted that we were old enough to be entrusted with performing some of Shakespeare's greatest work, and could also get Shakespeare—comprehend both the text and subtext, the language and poetry and narrative. I remember, too, a sense of trust among the students, and kind of camaraderie or esprit de corps. These aspects of trust, and being trusted, made me feel more adult."

David Medaris, in Carole Cox's fourth/fifth-grade class at
Shorewood Hills Elementary, Madison, Wisconsin, 1968–1969, and
"Shakespeare for Kids" summer program, 1971, 1972, and 1973

As I think FDR said, people often forget the details of human interaction, but they remember how the interaction made them feel. As someone who literally came from the other side of the tracks, and as someone whose world experiences were very different from most of those in the group, I have nothing but fond and warm feelings for the experience. Everyone, starting with you, was always welcoming and treated me like a "local." Those two summers with your group were among the best experiences I had growing up in Madison.

More specifically, I do remember the long bike rides to practice. But I always looked forward to the ride, as the payoff was easily worth it. I remember the performances on the front lawn of Wendy Harper's home—it was magical and felt like a time machine back to Shakespeare's time. And one specific memory I have of you, besides all of the wonderful direction and advice you provided along the way, is that of you nursing your baby after rehearsals when we were "hanging around". I really knew I was not in "Kansas" anymore, and that I had entered a more interesting and progressive place that did not exist in my experience. I have been hanging around more interesting and progressive places ever since.

Tim Riddiough, in Carole Cox's "Shakespeare for Kids" summer program,
Madison Wisconsin, 1973 and 1974

# REFERENCES

Cox, C. 2008. *Teaching Language Arts: A Student-Centered Classroom.* 6th ed. New York: Pearson/Allyn & Bacon.

Cox, C., and P. Boyd-Batstone. 2009. *Engaging English Learners: Exploring Literature, Developing Literacy, and Differentiating Instruction.* New York: Pearson/Allyn & Bacon.

International Reading Association (IRA) and National Council of Teachers of English (NCTE). 1996. *Standards for the English language arts.* Newark, DE: IRA; Urbana, IL: NCTE.

National Institute of Child Health and Human Development (NICHD). 2000. *Report of the National Reading Panel: Teaching Children to Read: An Evidence-based Assessment of the Scientific Research Literature on Reading and Its Implications for Reading Instruction.* NIH Publication NO. 00-4769. Washington, DC: U.S. Government Printing Office.

# CHAPTER 2

## Choosing a Play

This chapter explains my criteria for choosing one of Shakespeare's plays to perform with children. I also list my top ten plays based on these selection criteria. Also included in the chapter are narratives of the stories of each of the plays, which may help you decide which play to choose, and which you can use to introduce the play you choose to children, as well as the special attractions I found each play holds for younger performers.

## CHOOSING A FIRST PLAY: *MACBETH* FOR MY FOURTH/FIFTH-GRADE CLASS

I didn't actually choose the first play I did with children, nor did I even choose to do Shakespeare, as you read in the introduction. My experience performing Shakespeare with children started with one issue of Scholastic's *Newstime*, a weekly newspaper for elementary students. It included a script for *Hamlet* that teacher Albert Cullum had adapted by condensing it to a reasonable length to be performed by children. Once my students shamed me into letting them perform it, we used his script.

We performed *Hamlet* in the fall. We were a smash. We immediately started talking about the next play we would do. We were addicted. Right before winter break, I promised them we would start a new play in January. Now I got to choose the play. I chose *Macbeth,* and *Macbeth* has become my favorite play to begin with children. It has several attractions. It's the shortest play by Shakespeare. It has swords, warriors, witches, a ghost, a battle, and bad words. We take a close look at good versus evil, and somebody goes crazy.

But different plays have different attractions. *Romeo and Juliet* is an open invitation to students to identify with characters not far from their own age and to experience feelings about others different than themselves. It also has swords and fights and dancing. *Julius Caesar* is good for a large class. It has several parts of similar size in the conspirators and a Roman mob. *A Midsummer Night's Dream* allows for cross-age grouping. Older students play royalty and young lovers, and younger students play fairies and workmen.

When you choose the play, also consider the number of students you will work with and the makeup of your class or group, as well as what you might be studying in class or what is going on in the world around you. The timeliness of Shakespeare's plays is, well, timeless. Here are the selection criteria that I developed for my own use over the years.

# CRITERIA FOR PLAY SELECTION

It was with that first *Macbeth* that I chose to do with my class that I began to develop criteria, which I refined over many years and many play productions with students. You may find other criteria that are important to you as well, or based on your own experience, but here are mine:

## I like the play and think my students would, too

It's a commitment for a teacher to do Shakespeare with children, and you as well as your students should like it. I liked *Macbeth* because it was Scottish, and so am I. My father's parents emigrated from Aberdeen right before World War I. My father played in the Chicago Highlanders bagpipe band when I was a child. Every Halloween I wore the little kilt my Grandma Rosie brought me from Scotland on one of her trips home to visit her brother Arthur, who lived in a veterans' home because of wounds he suffered as a soldier in the Gordon Highlanders during World War I. I still have relatives there, and I still get chills of delight at the sound of a bagpipe. I thought my students would like the medieval Scottish setting, the witches and ghost, the battles, and the classic battle between good and evil.

## The ideas and theme are appropriate and accessible to children

As in *Star Wars*, we know the good guys from the bad guys in *Macbeth*. It is a classic tale of a struggle between good and evil, heroes and villains. On another level, it also shows how a brave and loyal warrior like Macbeth can become cowardly and commit treason by murdering the king who trusted and rewarded him. It's the same duality found in the character of Darth Vader and many of the heroes in mythology and literature: Satan is a fallen angel in Milton's *Paradise Lost*. I felt that children could develop an understanding of the complexities inherent in such an archetypal character.

## There are characters children want to play

*Macbeth* had it all, I thought: kings, a queen, princes, brave warriors, lords and ladies of the court, a ghost, witches, and for good measure—two murderers. I have found that the supernatural plays well with children. They like to play ghosts, witches, fairies, and monsters. They also like warriors, clowns, drunks, and murderers. The more normal behaving characters are not always as prized.

## There are several parts of equal size and importance, and some of the parts can be split, or the number of parts should be adaptable to the size of your groups

This is an idea I had that worked well with the first class, which I used again and again when I had a class of 30 or more students, or a summer group with 20 or more. By splitting the parts of Macbeth and Lady Macbeth before and after the murder of King Duncan, two children could play each one. I did the same with the witches. They appear in two scenes (it can be three in a longer version for older students), so six or even nine children can be witches. The lords and ladies and princes and warriors parts seemed to have relatively equal importance, so all students would have a good part to play. See chapter 3 for more on how to match the number of students to the number of parts and achieve a good balance for participation by all students.

I believe every child should have a part in the play and feel good about that part. All of them can help with the stagecraft, but I don't like the idea that some children are on the stage while others remain behind it. Shakespeare is ideal for this. Sometimes the smallest parts, such as a ghost, fairy, or a comic character, are the parts children like best.

## The play has action and a fast-moving plot

*Macbeth* hits the ground running as Macbeth and Banquo return from the battle field and encounter the three witches, who make the fateful prophesy that Macbeth will be king. The plot unfolds quickly from there, with plotting, deception, multiple murders, and Lady Macbeth's descent into madness and suicide, and there is a huge battle scene at the end. It is the shortest of Shakespeare's plays, full of nonstop action

## Tragedy is easier for children than comedy

Macbeth and Lady Macbeth create mayhem, and I have found that children can carry this off. Most of us would agree that regicide and murdering innocent women and children in the play is tragic, not to mention Lady Macbeth's descent into madness. But comedy is more subtle and elusive and harder for children to portray, especially if it is language based or relies on innuendo, including sexual innuendo, which Shakespeare frequently used. Children do well with comedies that rely more on broad, physical humor and slapstick.

## Consider how you will deal with staging and weapons in a play that has sword fights or a battle scene

*Macbeth* has a battle scene between armies and an individual fight scene between Macbeth and Macduff. I decided that we would not use fake-looking cardboard swords. I wanted children to feel proud and in character, and I didn't think that was likely to occur if they were in a battle scene waving pieces of cardboard at each other. I discovered several ways to find and make realistic, safe prop weapons (described in chapter 6). There are ways to stage fights and battles in a stylized fashion that would not require realistic prop weapons, and even offstage, even though Shakespeare did not intend these scenes to be played offstage. In my experience, however, children really want to play these scenes, and they throw themselves into them with great energy. They take some effort to stage and practice, but I always felt the students' engagement in the play rehearsals and performing were well worth it. If you don't want to go beyond cardboard for prop weapons, avoid plays with fights and battles. There are great comedies you could do instead.

"Shakespeare for Kids" was always a great opportunity to see my friends during the summer in something that was structured and fun. Looking back, it certainly beat generic summer camp, which I'm glad I don't know anything about. Canoe rides and afternoon crafts never looked all that fun.

I also have a definite favorite Shakespeare play of all the five plays that I did: *Macbeth*. I don't know what exactly about the play draws me to it. Maybe it's the Scottishness, or the cool atmosphere and murder plots. I do remember it having the best fight scenes, especially because we got to use swords and shields with some weight to them. Not like the lighter rapiers from *Romeo and Juliet*.

Gordon Spates, in Carole Cox's "Shakespeare for Kids" summer program in
Long Beach, California, 1991, 1992, 1993, 1994, 1995, and 1996

## Match the play to your class or group of students

Consider your class or group of students when you choose a play. There are many factors that could be important. First is the number of students in your class. Some plays, like *Julius Caesar* or *A Midsummer Night's Dream*, have more parts to cast. If you choose another play with a smaller cast, think about how you can use some of the strategies described in chapter 3 for splitting parts to increase the number of students who have a part.

Consider the age of your students, but don't be limited by it. I have done most of the ten plays described here with different age groups, and some plays—especially *A Midsummer Night's Dream*—with a cross-age cast, from pre-kindergarten/kindergarten to upper elementary age.

Also consider ways to integrate Shakespeare into your own curriculum. For example, choose *Julius Caesar* for a class study of Greek mythology in fifth grade or a social studies class on the ancient world in sixth to eighth grades. Choose a play with a European setting, such as *Macbeth, Hamlet*, or *Richard III* if you are studying European or world history. Choose *The Tempest* or *A Midsummer Night's Dream* if you are doing a unit on fantasy literature in class, or *The Comedy of Errors* or *The Taming of the Shrew* if you are doing a unit on humorous literature. *Twelfth Night* links beautifully to the study of music and song.

There are plays I have never done because they don't meet these criteria, in general, or have more adult themes that I decided might not play well with children. Others might disagree, but I have never done *Othello* for the latter reason, and also because there is very little action in it. The play is mostly conversations, and the battle scenes take place offstage. I find Iago chilling, and I'm not sure I understand his jealousy and malevolence. I was never prepared to take on *The Merchant of Venice* and the anti-Semitism in the play. *King Lear* is very, very old, at the end of his life, something I thought might not resonate with children as much as aspects of other characters. In some plays I thought there might be too little action, for example *As You Like It* and *Much Ado About Nothing*.

The only history play I have ever done is *Richard III*. Oh, what a villain! But we empathize with him, too, and the plot moves well. I also did this play with a group of students of whom at least one had already done the other plays I would have chosen, so we tried it and liked it. I've also never done plays whose characters rely heavily on sexual innuendo, such as Falstaff in *Henry V*. Although Queen Elizabeth I loved Falstaff in *Henry V* and asked Shakespeare to write another play with this character in it—*The Merry Wives of Windsor*—apparently humor at the time was bawdy, and Elizabeth I ruled the country but did not teach elementary school children.

# MY TOP TEN PLAYS BY SHAKESPEARE FOR CHILDREN

These are the plays I have performed with children. There is a narrative of the story of the play for each as well as a discussion of the special attractions each play offers, based on my experience doing them with children. Different plays have different attractions.

1. *Macbeth*

2. *Hamlet*

3. *Romeo and Juliet*

4. *Julius Caesar*

5. *A Midsummer Night's Dream*

6. *The Comedy of Errors*

7. *The Taming of the Shrew*

8. *Twelfth Night*

9. *The Tempest*

10. *Richard III*

## *Macbeth*

### *The Story of the Play*

The setting is eighth-century Scotland, and King Duncan rules the country, which has been at war. A great battle takes place before the play starts, and we first see Macbeth and Banquo, generals in King Duncan's army, returning home after a great victory for Scotland. They are on the moors, at night, when they meet three witches, who make a prophecy: Macbeth will be the Thane of Glamis and king, and Banquo's son will be king.

The witches disappear, leaving the two men perplexed. Macbeth writes a letter to Lady Macbeth telling her of the prophesy, and she wonders if they should help make it come true. Upon returning to the Scottish court, King Duncan rewards Macbeth by making him Thane of Glamis. It seems the witches' prophecy is coming true. Lady Macbeth tells Macbeth that they should kill Duncan so the prophecy will indeed come true. Macbeth will be king. He hesitates, but at her urging he murders Duncan and makes it appear as if his servants have done it. He is declared king.

Duncan's sons and the rightful heirs to the throne, Malcolm and Donalbain, become afraid and flee to England. Macbeth hires two murderers to kill Banquo and his son, Fleance, to prevent that part of the prophecy from coming true, but although they kill Banquo, Fleance escapes. Banquo's ghost comes back to haunt Macbeth, and he and Lady Macbeth become afraid. Macbeth orders the death of anyone he thinks will threaten his right to the throne. Many noblemen flee to England, including Macduff, and Macbeth orders his wife and children murdered. Lady Macbeth begins her descent into madness, haunted by the blood she feels is on her hands.

In England, Macduff learns of the murder of his wife and children and joins forces with other Scottish nobles in exile there and the English general Siward. Macbeth is afraid and visits the witches again to ask them what the future has in store. They tell him that no man born of a woman can harm him and that he need not be afraid until Birnam Wood comes to high Dunsinane Hill, where his castle sits. Meanwhile, Lady Macbeth throws herself off the castle wall and dies.

In the final battle, the allied English and Scottish forces, led by Macduff, hide behind tree branches cut from Birnam Wood as they attack the castle. Nonetheless, Macbeth faces Macduff fearlessly and tells him that he leads a charmed life—no man born of a woman can harm him. Macduff tells Macbeth that his charm is useless because he was not truly born of a woman in the usual way. (He was born by what we now call cesarean section.). Macbeth now knows his fate but fearlessly cries out to Macduff, "Lay on Macduff and damned be him that first cries 'hold, enough'." Macduff kills him in the fight and cuts off his head. Malcolm, the exiled prince, is hailed as the new king of Scotland.

## *Special Attractions*

I chose *Macbeth* as the first play I adapted for two reasons: it's Scottish, and it's short. This play really moves quickly, right from the chance meeting of Macbeth and Banquo with the witches on the moors at night, who make the prophecy that Macbeth will be king. When condensing it for children, you can easily choose the scenes that contain action and tell the story. It has a real-time quality, and one scene leads quickly into the next to tell the story. There are plenty of good characters to play, so everyone in a class of 30 may have an interesting part. By splitting the parts of Macbeth and Lady Macbeth before and after the murder of King Duncan, and having three different witches appear in their two scenes, you can cast ten children in these juicy parts. We also see a clear distinction between good and evil, at first. Macbeth and Lady Macbeth appear villainous but are conflicted as well, which makes for interesting questions leading to discussions about why Macbeth betrayed his king. Was it the prophecy? Was it Lady Macbeth urging him on? Is she the real villain? Was it a thirst for power? Or was it simply inevitable that the prophecy of the witches would be fulfilled, that everything was determined by fate? There are also strong women in this play in the characters of Lady Macbeth and the witches. They have power and a strong male side, which makes for interesting and contemporary ambivalence that is not lost on children. I was amazed to learn how much supernatural characters appealed to children. This play has both the witches and Banquo's ghost. Children also seem to understand the contrast between evil—in the Macbeths and the murderers—and innocence—in Macduff's wife and children. There is a hero in Macduff, although the ambivalence is there as well, as he abandons his wife and children, who are subsequently murdered on Macbeth's orders. The battle is appealing, especially because it has a trick, a reverse Trojan horse. To camouflage the approach to the castle, the English army cuts branches to hide themselves so that it appears that the forest is moving. Macbeth also has knives, swords, blood, and bad words in the safety and lofty environs of the theater.

The play *Macbeth* shows that sometimes neither good nor bad wins. The witches got their way, and so did Macduff. Macduff was also a general. At one point, Macbeth and Macduff were friends. Then Macbeth kills Macduff's wife and babies. In the end Macduff kills Macbeth to avenge his wife and babies.

Macbeth was a good man basically. He was the king's favorite, and he was a leader among men. His downfall came because he was influenced by his wife. She made him do the evil things he did. Sometimes even good people can be pushed to the limit.

Joey, nine years old, playing Macbeth in Carole Cox's "Shakespeare for Kids" summer program, Baton Rouge, Louisiana, 1982

# Hamlet

## The Story of the Play

Hamlet is the Prince of Denmark. His father has died suddenly, and his mother, Queen Gertrude, has quickly married his uncle, Claudius, his father's brother. Claudius is now the King of Denmark and Hamlet's stepfather. Hamlet is unhappy about his father's death and confused by his mother's marriage to his uncle so soon after his father died. When his friend Horatio tells him that he has seen the Ghost of Hamlet's father on the castle walls, Hamlet is impatient to see for himself and try to learn how his father died. The Ghost tells him that he was murdered by his brother, Hamlet's uncle Claudius, now King of Denmark. Claudius poured poison in his ear when he was sleeping in an orchard. He did it so he could become king. Hamlet vows that he will find out if this is true, and he pretends madness while he does. His mother, Claudius, and Polonius tell Ophelia, Polonius's daughter, to talk to him while they eavesdrop so they can discover the source of his madness.

Some traveling Players come to the castle, and Hamlet has them act out a scene in which someone poisons a king sleeping in an orchard, a "play within a play." He wants to see how Claudius reacts to this, and when the latter becomes very agitated, Hamlet is convinced of his guilt. His mother is upset and calls him to her room, where Polonius is hiding behind a curtain to eavesdrop. Hamlet tells his mother what the ghost has said and is angry with her, but the Ghost appears again and tells him not to hurt his mother. Only Hamlet sees the Ghost, so Gertrude is now convinced he is truly mad. The hidden Polonius makes a sound; Hamlet draws his sword and kills the old man behind the curtain, thinking it is Claudius. Ophelia, mad with grief over the death of Polonius, drowns herself. Claudius convinces Ophelia's brother Laertes, an excellent swordsman whom Hamlet admires, to challenge Hamlet to a fencing match. But Hamlet will not know that Laertes's sword is really poisoned, and Laertes will be able to avenge the death of both his father and his sister. To be sure Hamlet dies, Claudius also puts a poisoned pearl in a drink for Hamlet during the match.

Hamlet suspects nothing, but after Laertes actually cuts Hamlet with the poisoned sword, their swords are accidentally switched, and Hamlet, angry that Laertes has drawn his blood, cuts Laertes with the poisoned sword. Claudius offers Hamlet the poisoned cup, but Gertrude takes it, without knowing it is poisoned, and drinks a toast to Hamlet. As he begins to weaken, Laertes tells Hamlet that they both are dying and that Claudius is to blame. Gertrude realizes she too is dying. Hamlet grabs the poisoned sword and plunges it into Claudius, avenging his father's death as he dies.

## Special Attractions

*Hamlet* was the first play I did with children, and perhaps because it was *Hamlet* and arguably Shakespeare's most famous play, it opened my eyes to the possibilities of doing Shakespeare with children, because they loved it so much and did it so well. Just by looking over the script, one of my students recognized Hamlet's doubts and confusion about many things in his life. The conflict between Hamlet and his mother Queen Gertrude seemed especially easy for this group of fourth- and fifth-grade students to understand as they approached adolescence. I never felt that any of the characters required much explanation. The students understood Polonious's paternal pomposity but also why his daughter Ophelia and son Laertes bonded together in the complex atmosphere of the court, and why they all loved and tried to protect each other. They understood Hamlet's buddy Horatio and their friendship. I think their favorite character was Hamlet's father's ghost. They also loved the gravediggers. This was my first inkling of how much students love to play supernatural and offbeat characters. When soliloquies and long exchanges between characters are condensed, the play moves well, and children understand the drama of the story. It is a bit more difficult to do with a larger group, because there are no armies as in *Macbeth* or Roman conspirators or mobs as in *Julius Caesar*. The number of parts can be increased with the characters of the traveling actors in the "play within the play," and I have found students very interested in producing this scene authentically, with music and dance and mime. Hamlet is a big part, and he appears in so many scenes that the part could be split. The parts of Queen Gertrude and King Claudius could also be split. There are court scenes, which can include any number of ladies and courtiers, but not a lot of lines for them to speak. The final fencing scene between Hamlet and Laertes is complex. It is supposedly for sport, but Laertes has secretly conspired with King Claudius to use a poisoned sword to kill Hamlet. There are many exchanges with swords, and Hamlet and Laertes, as well as Gertrude and Claudius, speak lines, so it should be carefully staged. Stage foils are really necessary, and not difficult to find, and careful staging is necessary because nearly all the main characters die in this scene. I have found that children take the play seriously and seriously want to perform Shakespeare's most well-known play well.

It is violent, full of dead people and fights. It is like the age of King Arthur with battles, Kings, Queens, and courtiers. When Hamlet wanted to settle something or anybody else they usually fought or were killed. It's a fascinating story of excitement and non-ending action. A fight means a fight 'til victory, no thoughts of missing the person, not caring for them—just victory.

> Amy, nine years old, playing the parts of Rosencrantz, Osric, and Players in Carole Cox's "Shakespeare for Kids" summer program, Baton Rouge, Louisiana, 1982

*Hamlet* is all about murder! And how to get even and die in the process. But my character doesn't die.

> Chris, 12 years old, playing Horatio in Carole Cox's "Shakespeare for Kids" summer program, Baton Rouge, Louisiana, 1982

# Julius Caesar

## The Story of the Play

Julius Caesar, a great Roman general, enters a public place with his wife Calpurnia, Brutus and Brutus's wife Portia, Cassius, Casca, and a great crowd following them. A Soothsayer in the crowd calls to Caesar that he should "Beware the ides of March." Later, Brutus and Cassius are talking when they hear the crowd shouting that they want Caesar to be their king. Brutus is a good friend of Caesar's, but Cassius tells him that Caesar is too ambitious.

Cassius conspires with Casca and others to assassinate Caesar before he gains too much power, and they convince Brutus to join them in the plot to kill him on March 15, the ides of March that Caesar was warned about by the Soothsayer. Portia knows her husband Brutus is troubled and begs him to confide in her, and Calpurnia tells her husband Caesar that he should not leave the house because she is afraid for him.

The next day Caesar enters the Capitol to speak to the Senators. Casca stabs Caesar, followed by the other conspirators, and finally by Brutus. People run in confusion as Caesar dies. At his funeral in front of a throng of Citizens, who demand to know why Caesar has been killed, Brutus speaks and tells that he was afraid Caesar would have too much power and that Romans would lose their freedom if he were king. Then Caesar's loyal friend Mark Antony speaks over Caesar's body.

In a stirring speech he convinces the Romans to mutiny against Brutus and the other conspirators and avenge Caesar's death.

## Special Attractions

This is a play that works well with all students, from the youngest to older ones. It's a good choice for a fifth- or sixth-grade class that might be doing a unit on Greek and Roman mythology, or for a sixth- to eighth-grade class studying the ancient world in social studies. The play might be performed in language arts in conjunction with social studies, in a block middle school schedule, for example. It can be done with a large class because it has many parts of equal size, such as the Roman conspirators against Caesar, and one character does not dominate the play. Caesar's role is not huge, as he is assassinated during the play. Two roles of relatively equal importance are Brutus and Mark Antony. Caesar's wife Calpurnia and Brutus's wife Portia each have good scenes. Although the play does not have any supernatural parts, the Soothsayer is a favorite among children.

It also can be staged simply in a classical style or in a contemporary fashion. The assassination scene can look stiff and awkward, so I made it more stylized, choreographed the knife thrusts with a drum beat, and added lighting effects—flicking lights on and off in time to the drum beats as well. I usually did not do the whole play, which continues after Mark Antony's speech with a civil war and battles between the forces of Mark Antony and those led by Brutus and the other conspirators. For younger students I ended it when the Roman mob rushes out to find and kill the conspirators after Mark Antony's moving speech over Caesar's body. I have also extended it to include the civil war when performing it with older students.

All of this makes for a play that lends itself to fairly easy staging and structure for success for children. It does not require weapons other than daggers for the conspirators who murder Caesar, and if you end with Mark Antony's oration, there are no fights or battle scenes. Costuming is also easy. Everyone wears a simple toga and sandals. Main characters can be color coded with a drape of cloth over the shoulder, such as purple for Caesar. Simple headpieces of plastic vines complete the look. It's a somber play about power and loyalty, dictatorship and democracy, but very manageable with children, even the youngest, and another good play to start Shakespeare with children.

I still remember my part by heart in *Julius Caesar* since I was the soothsayer and I had only one line: "Caesar, beware the Ides of March!" I practiced and practiced that line until I had it down. When I had my 30 seconds on stage and delivered my line in true Shakespearean fashion, I might add, my sister, who was about two at the time, called out "That's Phillip. That's my brother!" Of course everyone heard it. You can imagine my embarrassment. I was scarred for life.

Phillip Shiman, third/fourth-grade student in Carole Cox's class at Shorewood Hills Elementary, Madison, Wisconsin, 1969–1970

# Romeo and Juliet

## The Story of the Play

In the city of Verona in Italy there are two feuding families, the Capulets and the Montagues, causing fighting and civil strife in the streets between members of each family as well as their servants. Romeo is the son of the head of the house of Montague, and his good friends are Benvolio and

Mercutio. They decide to go in disguise to a masked ball given by the head of the house of Capulet, whose daughter is Juliet. At the ball, Romeo and Juliet meet. Romeo secretly goes to her house under cover of night, and they speak of their love for each other. Romeo tells her to send her nurse to meet him the next day so he can send her a message about where and what time they can be married by Friar Laurence.

The next day Juliet's cousin Tybalt, famous for his swordsmanship and temper, gets in a fight with Mercutio and kills him after Romeo will not fight him because he is Juliet's cousin and they are now secretly married. Romeo sees his friend die on his behalf, challenges Tybalt to fight, and kills him. Escalus, the Prince of Verona, banishes Romeo and warns that if there is any more fighting between the Capulets and the Montagues, the penalty will be death. Romeo flees to Mantua.

Meanwhile, Lord Capulet has arranged for his daughter Juliet to marry Paris, but she refuses because she is already secretly married to Romeo. Her father and mother are very angry, and the wedding is planned despite her protests. She goes to Friar Laurence to find out what to do; he gives her a potion that will make her fall into a deep sleep and appear to be dead. He tells her he will send a messenger to Romeo to tell him to secretly return to Verona and rescue her from the family tomb, where she will be buried. But the messenger is unable to reach Romeo, who hears instead that Juliet is dead. He gets some poison from an apothecary, returns to Verona, and enters the Capulet tomb, where he takes poison and dies near Juliet's body. Juliet awakes from the deep sleep caused by the potion she took, sees Romeo's body, and kills herself with his dagger. When the families come together at the tomb, they vow they will never fight again.

## *Special Attractions*

Younger and older children love this play. They seem to intuitively understand the basic intergenerational conflict between parents and authority and children and the recklessness of youth. I think the variety of contrasting parts appeals to them, starting with the Capulets versus the Montagues. I think they also enjoy the flamboyant Renaissance costuming, with long dresses and ball gowns and headpieces for the girls and vests and capes and hats with the colors of either the Capulets or the Montagues for the male parts.

There are several sword fights with Renaissance rapiers, camaraderie among the groups of young men, and a dose of comedy with Juliet's nurse and the servants. It also moves quickly, from one fateful event to the next. I always include a simple dance in the scene for the Capulet's ball, and I have found that even if a character is not in that scene, we vary their costumes so they can go to the ball, because they all want to go to the ball and dance. There are several possible fight scenes between members of the two feuding clans; these can be staged with children drawing their weapons, brandishing them at each other, and crossing blades once or twice. Two fights are important. The first is between Tybalt and Mercutio, who dies. The second is between Romeo and Tybalt, who dies. These can be quite simple but do require stage weapons.

I did this play in Long Beach, California, with a group of fourth- and fifth-grade students, including two English learners, not long after the 1992 Los Angeles riots. It was clear from their comments, conversations, and our group discussions that they saw the connections between the play about the tragic consequences of the family feud in Renaissance Verona, Italy, and the racial conflict among white, African American, and Korean American communities in Los Angeles after the announcement of the innocent verdict in the trial of police officers who were charged with beating Rodney King, an African American. This is not to suggest children don't enjoy the play. They do, from servants insulting each other on the streets of Verona to the playfulness between Juliet and her old nurse, to the Capulet's masked ball, and of course, the fights. But they also seem to grasp the theme of hatred and intolerance of others who are different that Shakespeare so skillfully addresses in the play.

Romeo and Juliet were enemies but they didn't know it. But still they loved each other. And their parents didn't find out until it was too late.

Faith, six years old, playing Lady Capulet in Carole Cox's "Shakespeare for Kids"
summer program, Baton Rouge, Louisiana, 1983

# A Midsummer Night's Dream

## The Story of the Play

King Theseus of Athens is set to marry Hippolyta, Queen of the Amazons, and the whole city will celebrate. Egeus comes to Theseus and asks for his help in forcing his daughter Hermia to marry Demetrius, the man he has chosen for her. She has refused because she is in love with Lysander, and she tells the King that Demetrius has wooed her friend Helena, who now loves him. An ancient law of Athens says that a girl must either marry the man her father has chosen or be put to death. Theseus concedes to this law. Hermia and Lysander secretly plan to run away from Athens together, but Helena overhears them, and to win his favor, she tells Demetrius. That night, all four of them end up in the woods outside Athens.

Hermia and Lysander are together, Demetrius follows them, and Helena follows him. This wood is enchanted and the home of the fairy king Oberon and the fairy queen Titania. Oberon is angry at Titania because she has a changeling child that he wants as a servant, but she will not give him up. Oberon and his henchman Puck conspire to get the child and take revenge on Titania, and also overhear Lysander and Demetrius fighting over Hermia. They feel pity for Helena, who is left out.

Oberon sends Puck around the world to find a magic flower, the juice of which when squeezed on a sleeping person's eyes will make that person love the first thing he or she sees upon waking. Oberon tells Puck to squeeze it on the sleeping Demetrius's eyes so he will fall in love with Helena, but he mistakes the sleeping Lysander for Demetrius, and when they wake up, they both see Helena and love her. Hermia is furious.

Meanwhile, a group of rustic workmen are in the woods to practice a play to perform at Theseus's wedding. Puck turns the workman Bottom into an ass and squeezes the magic flower juice on the sleeping Titania's eyes. When she wakes up she falls in love with Bottom, even though he has the head of an ass. Through magic, Oberon and Puck finally sort things out with the young lovers so that Lysander again loves Hermia and Demetrius now loves Helena. Oberon takes the spell off Titania after she gives him her changeling child. The rustic workmen perform their "tragical/comical" play *Pyramus and Thisbe* for the wedding of Theseus and Hippolyta, Hermia and Lysander, and Demetrius and Helena. At midnight Oberon, Titania, Puck, and all the fairies slip into the palace and bless everyone in it.

## Special Attractions

I love performing this play with children. Although the play includes an ancient Greek hero, an Amazon queen, and a forest full of fairies, the characters are all so very human, behaving in ways that children recognize, that their actions are clearly understood. The themes of love, friendship, conflict with authority, loyalty, disobedience, selfishness, trickery, and finally harmony and a happy ending are very accessible to students. There are many wonderful, different types of characters for children to play, including supernatural fairies and a man turned into an ass by magic, a king and queen, rustic buffoons, and four young people who get into a lot of arguments. What's not to like?

This play can work with a large group because there are so many interesting parts of equal size. If you have a smaller group, the parts of Theseus and Hippolyta and Oberon and Titania can be played by the same children. It is also the absolute best play for cross-age or cross-grade groups, if this is a special project in a school with team teaching and integrated projects, or in a recreational program in which you might have students of different ages. The oldest students can play Theseus and Hippolyta and Oberon and Titania as well as the four young lovers. The rustic workmen can be played by students the same age or younger. Even younger students can be Puck, and the youngest can be fairies. I have performed this play with fourth/fifth graders as the human and fairy royalty and with a pre-K fairy and several fairies in kindergarten and first grade. This was in a recreational program, and younger siblings of the older students wanted to participate. I worried at first about their ability to be quiet offstage and make their cues, but they were actually the most serious and best-behaved cast members. They did not want to do anything to jeopardize their chance to be in a play with their big brothers and sisters. And they actually showed them up. This play also really moves quickly and is very well constructed among the different sets of characters. The play by the rustics is almost a separate piece and usually a show-stopper, with its ridiculous lines and broad comedy. All the fights are verbal, except when Lysander and Demetrius draw their swords in the forest fighting over Helena; because it is damp and misty and they are under a spell, they usually can't even find each other. In my experience with children, this is less a romantic play than you might think and more a playful one. It's just fun. Added pleasures are the beautiful language and songs of the fairies and places to add music and dance. It's a magical romp in an enchanted wood, and I've taken children there many times.

*A Midsummer Night's Dream* is about six people who have marital problems and it takes a bunch of fairies to solve their problems for them.

Christopher, eight years old, playing Oberon in Carole Cox's "Shakespeare for Kids"
summer program, Baton Rouge, Louisiana, 1983

# The Comedy of Errors

## The Story of the Play

Aegeon, a merchant of the city of Ephesus, and Emilia are the parents of twin sons, both named Antipholus. Another set of twin brothers, both named Dromio, are taken in by the family to be the servants of the two Antipholuses. While the twins are still babies, the family is shipwrecked at sea and separated. Aegeon and one twin and his servant land in Syracuse, and Emilia and the other twin and his servant land in Ephesus. After many years, Aegeon returns to Ephesus to look for his other son, but he is arrested and put in jail because the two cities have a law against anyone from the other town entering either town. Aegeon is condemned to death by the Duke.

Antipholus and Dromio of Syracuse come to Ephesus seeking Antipholus of Ephesus. There is much confusion, however, between the masters and the servants, who mistake one for the other and are never in the same place at the same time. Adriana, wife of Antipholus of Ephesus, and her sister Luciana also mistake the twins and twin servants for each other, as does everybody else. Adriana mistakes her husband's twin for her husband, Luciana thinks her brother-in-law is courting her, and the servants get beatings because it appears they are not following an order that was actually given to the other one.

In the end, everything is explained and everyone is reunited. Emilia, who is now an Abbess in a convent, is reunited with her husband, Aegeon, who is pardoned by the Duke. Antipholus of Ephesus and his wife Adriana, Antipholus of Syracuse and Luciana, and the two Dromios meet as brothers for the first time.

## Special Attractions

*The Comedy of Errors* is another good play to choose for the youngest students. It is based on Roman comedy. The mistaken identity and slapstick play well with children. There are many parts of equal importance because the main characters are two sets of twins—masters and servants. If you split the four parts, eight children can play main parts.

The play is fast paced as the mistaken identity leads the characters from one silly situation to another. This play has sometimes reminded me of *I Love Lucy*. I think this is the easiest of comedies for children to carry off because the humor is so broad, and the audience is always in on the joke of the two masters who are twins with two servants who are twins, but each master and servant has been separated from the other since birth, and they are now coincidentally brought together in the same town. There is a lot of running around and chases, as well as feigned beatings of servants. Costumes can be simple classical or of any era, and simple or fun and fanciful. There is some poignancy in the ending in a scene with the Abbess, really the mother of both Antipholuses, and when everyone is reunited or united, it's a happy and satisfying ending.

# The Taming of the Shrew

## The Story of the Play

In Padua, Italy, a rich gentleman named Baptista has two unmarried daughters. The oldest is Katharina (Kate), who has a reputation for being difficult to get along with, or a "shrew." The younger daughter is Bianca, who has suitors who want to marry her: Gremio, an old gentleman, and Hortensio. Baptista will not allow Bianca to marry until her older sister Kate is married. A young man from Pisa named Lucentio, son of Vincentio, comes to Padua to study and falls in love with Bianca. He poses as her tutor, and they both trick Bianca's two suitors and her father.

Bianca's suitors realize that in order for one of them to marry Bianca, they have to find a husband for Kate. They find Petruchio, who agrees to court Kate, knowing that she has a large dowry and he would like the money. Kate agrees to marry him, but Petruchio arrives at the wedding dressed in outlandish clothes and behaving wildly and irrationally. He is determined to tame Kate, whom he hopes will be more agreeable to get him to stop.

Meanwhile, Bianca and Lucentio, who have secretly plotted to be married, can now tell Baptista of their wishes because Kate is married. Kate goes to Petruchio's home in the country, where he continues his bizarre behavior. Kate becomes more agreeable because she wants Petruchio to allow her to get new clothes and go to Bianca's wedding in Padua. At the wedding, Kate proves to be a more pleasant and devoted wife than Bianca or Hortensio's new wife and lectures them on how a woman should behave toward a husband.

## Special Attractions

This play is fun and lively, and there is never a dull moment. I like the carefully drawn characters, who at first appear one dimensional, for example, Kate the Shrew and Petruchio the opportunist who needs to marry for money. But both of them begin to reveal other sides of themselves in their interactions with each other. This may be a play to choose for an older group, with the emphasis on the battle of the sexes, to do after you have already done a play and students have some experience, or to do when you are studying the Renaissance.

However, I have also done this as a first play with a group of eight- to ten-year-olds, who absolutely romped through it, relishing the tension between Kate and her father, meek and sneaky sister Bianca, Bianca's suitors, and the verbal sparring between Kate and just about everyone. I never felt they didn't understand what was going on in the scene after the marriage, when Petruchio is bent on "taming the shrew" by making her admit that it is first the sun and then the moon in the sky—or whatever he claims it to be. Children too live in the world of adult relationships, and I think they bring experience to understanding the dynamics between Petruchio and Kate.

Although Petruchio and Kate are the main parts and could be split before and after the wedding to accommodate a larger group, there are many other juicy parts as well. Petruchio's servant Grumio is a favorite and could also be split, as could the frustrated father and the ridiculous suitors for Bianca's hand. Bianca and Lucentio and the story of their secret romance while he pretends to be her tutor rather than suitor are also favorite parts. There just isn't a boring part in this play. To expand some of the smaller parts, characters may participate in the wedding scene and celebration, as well as the final homecoming celebration in the final scene. I usually add music, dancing, and lots of "business" in these scenes so children with smaller speaking parts can be entertainers if they have a special talent, or they can do research and find something that was done at Renaissance events, like juggling, and learn to do it.

This play moves really well, and there is excitement in every scene, most notably because of the presence of Kate—at first the tempestuous shrew and then the accommodating wife who genuinely seems to love her husband, as he does her. The subplots are lively and keep the play engaging as well: the suitors vying for the younger sister Bianca's hand and the plots to win her, as well as the secret romance between her and the "tutor" they send to speak well of her—actually a nobleman smitten with her, who tricks them to get into her presence.

The comedy in this play is easy to play. Children understand characters like Kate—argumentative, angry, and demanding—and the insecurity that often underlies this type of behavior. Watch them out in the schoolyard. They know who the bullies are and how to avoid them or make friends with them. Petruchio's preadolescent male behavior around Kate at first is completely recognizable. To get a girl's attention, act like a jerk. To get her to like you, give her presents and try not to act quite so much like a jerk. Weapons can be worn as part of a costume, and they are brandished a few times, but there are no real fights—only the verbal ones between Kate and just about everybody else.

Hear ye! Hear ye! Get in your houses! Lock your doors! Watch out for the taming of the shrew!

Kristin, ten years old, playing the Widow, and creator of the play program on which this was printed, in Carole Cox's "Shakespeare for Kids" summer program, Madison, Wisconsin, 1972

## Twelfth Night

### The Story of the Play

Duke Orsino of Illyria is in love with Olivia, a rich countess, but she is not in love with him. She is in mourning for her father and brother, both of whom have recently died, and does not want to be in the company of any men. On the seacoast, a young woman named Viola and her brother Sebastian have been in a shipwreck and the brother is feared lost. A sea captain rescues Viola off the coast of Illyria. She is alone, so she decides to disguise herself as a young man named Cesario and serve Duke Orsino.

Olivia has an uncle, Sir Toby Belch, who introduces her to the foolish Sir Andrew Aguecheek, who wants to marry her. Her grumpy steward Malvolio would like to marry her, too. Duke Orsino sends his new servant Cesario, really Viola in male disguise, to tell Olivia that he loves her. She is not interested in the Duke but is very drawn to Cesario (really Viola). Maria, who works for Olivia; Sir Toby Belch; Sir Andrew Aguecheek; and a Clown do not like Malvolio and trick him into thinking Olivia loves him by writing a letter pretending to be her. He makes a fool of himself in front of Olivia.

Meanwhile, Viola's brother Sebastian, who has not really been lost at sea, meets Olivia, who thinks he is Cesario/Viola, and they are married. Olivia sees Cesario/Viola and thinks it her husband; she is confused when Cesario/Viola says she does not love her. Finally, Viola tells the Duke she is really a woman and that she loves him, Olivia finds out that she has really married Viola's brother Sebastian, and everyone is happy.

## Special Attractions

I love the elegance of this play and the subtle treatment of gender identity through the device of disguise. The language is beautiful, and there are many songs, so music and dance may be added. I have only done this play with sixth to eighth graders, but that doesn't mean it wouldn't be successful with younger students. I would probably not do it as a first play, but each teacher has to make that decision independently. The first time I did it, one of the parents, who directed a boy's choir in Madison, Wisconsin, and whose son was in the play, helped him research tunes that could be used so the words could be sung. He and others sang with her help, and we staged the play with this feature in mind. I remember it as an enchanted production.

The ideas are accessible, if slightly confusing at first. I found children loved all the confusion and deception. We had many interesting discussions about gender and how people perceive us and the way we act and dress—these are themes preadolescents and adolescents are dealing with every day and often struggling to understand.

The main parts are unusually balanced in this play. There are no extremes, except Malvolio, the foppish and pathetic suitor, and children love to play him. There are also some comical servants they like—Fabian and a Clown. The main parts (Duke, Olivia, and Viola) could be split so six children could play them.

The plot is not fast paced and is more character than event driven, but it is always interesting. The comedy is subtle, unless you don't think it subtle that a woman is lovesick over a girl she thinks is a boy and a man is attracted to a girl he thinks is a boy. There are no blockbuster scenes, but rather one charming scene after another as we see the mystery play out. There are no fights, and no weapons are needed, except as costume pieces. For some reason I decided to add tiny white lights to the setting of the play because it takes place in winter. The music, song, and festive quality make it a beautiful play to perform with children.

# The Tempest

## The Story of the Play

A ship at sea is in a terrible storm, and even though the Master of the Ship, the Boatswain, and the Mariners try to stay afloat and save the passengers—Alonso, Ferdinand, Sebastian, Antonio, and Gonzalo—the ship is wrecked on an island. The island is the home of Prospero, who is the rightful Duke of Milan in exile, and his daughter Miranda, who only knows life on the island, where she has lived since she was three. Miranda is afraid her father, who is also a powerful wizard, has caused the storm. He tells her for the first time that he was the Duke of Milan, but while he spent his time studying, another man took over the city. Prospero was forced to flee in a boat with his baby daughter

Miranda. They came to the island; Gonzalo brought the Duke food, water, and his books, then returned to Milan.

The island is magic. Prospero is master of the spirit Ariel, who helped cause the storm but kept all the passengers and the ship safe. Caliban is a monster, whose mother was the witch Sycorax, and he must now obey Prospero. Ariel becomes invisible and sings a song to Ferdinand, the King's son, who is wandering the island after the shipwreck. Miranda sees him, and he falls in love with her, but Prospero is angry and puts a spell on him because he is the son of the Duke of Milan. Ariel is tricking the other passengers on another part of the island.

Caliban encounters Trinculo and Stephano, who are drinking; they torment him, and then all get drunk. Caliban swears to serve them, and they plot to take the island from Prospero. On another part of the island, Prospero is invisible and creates the illusion of a banquet for the shipwrecked passengers, then puts a charm on them. All the passengers are finally reunited; Prospero tells his story and gives up magic. Miranda and Ferdinand are together, and they will all return to Milan. Prospero frees Ariel.

## Special Attractions

My students loved the magic and the freedom of this play. I have done this play with both younger and older students, and each production was unique. One summer we staged the shipwreck scene with long strips of blue and green fabric held at each end by children, who waved them up and down in different patterns to look like waves. We were outside and used two hoses backstage to spray the scene, thunder and lightning sound effects, and lots of yelling by the Boatswain and the Mariners as they tried to save the ship. The students were totally engaged and kept adding to this scene right up to the time of performance.

There is no dominant part. Prospero is important, and he does cause a storm at sea, but he is an old man in a cape and a wizard's hat. Miranda and Fernando are charming, but there are many other interesting, even quirky parts: Ariel the spirit, Caliban the hideous monster, and Trinculo and Stephano who get drunk with Caliban. Antonio, Sebastian, and the other Lords appear in several scenes and have magic spells cast on them. I could tell children were really having fun with this play.

They also loved the magical banquet scene with the many spirits and tried to figure out how to make food appear to be floating. I found they really got into the spirit of the mysterious mood of this play. There are also songs, and music may be added. The sound and special effects of magic are left up to the imagination of the students, because after all, everything does take place on an enchanted island.

# Richard the III

## The Story of the Play

Richard, Duke of Gloucester, plots to take the throne of England, which King Edward IV is heir to after King Henry VI dies. There is a prophecy that says "G" will take Edward's throne and murder his heirs. George, Duke of Clarence, and brother of the new king, is imprisoned because of this prophecy, and Richard plots to set George against the king and to marry the Lady Anne, even though he has killed her husband and her father. He sends two murderers to kill Clarence in prison.

King Edward becomes sick and dies, and Richard becomes the protector of Edward's two young sons, who are now the heirs to the throne. He has married the Lady Anne. With the help of Lord Buckingham he kills anybody who stands in his way. He has the two young princes smothered as they sleep in the Tower of London. Buckingham finally becomes afraid for his own life and flees.

An army led by the Duke of Richmond is raised against the tyrant Richard. Before the battle, Richard sees the ghost of the people he has killed in his sleep. He feels fear before the battle and when he faces the opposing army. His horse is killed, but he fights Richmond on foot and is killed.

## *Special Attractions*

I have found that children are fascinated with Richard and his plotting and the murders of just about everybody. There is a good balance of parts among all the royalty and lords and ladies, and the play moves quickly from one bit of Richard's treachery to the next. I worried about doing a play with such a dominant main character, but I carefully condensed the script to give other characters speaking lines, and I have always found that the child who wanted to be Richard was up to the part.

There are interesting things to learn about the real historical events the play is based on and how Shakespeare revised them to discredit the Plantagenets, the royal line in England before the Tudors, the family of Queen Elizabeth I. There was always a question about how Henry VI, a Tudor, really became king, and whether he was a legitimate monarch. Evidently Shakespeare demonized Richard III, making him the fascinating monster in the play, to make the Tudor line, which defeated him in battle, appear legitimate.

## A Final Word on Choosing a Play

Children don't care as long as it's Shakespeare.

# CHAPTER 3

# Condensing a Play

This chapter takes you through a step-by-step process for condensing a play for children that would take about 30 to 45 minutes to perform. I never change Shakespeare's language and have never found this to be a problem. I describe how to condense the play by reducing characters, subplots, and soliloquies, with suggestions for different grade levels and groups of children, and revising the script during the rehearsal of the play if needed.

## LEAVE SHAKESPEARE'S LANGUAGE ALONE

My approach to performing Shakespeare with children has been to condense the play from the original, which might take two hours or more to perform, to a script that could be performed by students in grades 3–8 in 30 to 45 minutes. This allows time to prepare and get into costumes, rehearse the whole play, debrief, and make plans for the next rehearsal, in about 1 to 1½ hours. It has also always seemed about the right amount of time to sustain the children's interest in doing it and the audience's interest in watching it.

However, I leave Shakespeare's language alone. It never occurred to me to change it, even though I know that there is a belief that it can be inaccessible, especially to children. My decision to leave Shakespeare's language alone when condensing one of his plays for children was based on my experience as a teacher.

I should be clear that I was certainly no Shakespeare expert when I began. I only vaguely remember reading excerpts of *Julius Caesar* in high school. I had only seen one of Shakespeare's plays at that time, a production of *Romeo and Juliet* at the Old Globe Theatre in San Diego when I was 22, when I began performing his plays with children. I do remember how beautiful the language sounded to me. And although it sounded different than modern English, I understood what was happening even if every word or phrase wasn't familiar to me. I was born in Chicago and grew up in southern California, going to schools where many students spoke a language other than English at home and often at school. I spent my junior year abroad in France and traveled all over Europe, the Middle East, the Soviet Union, and North Africa. Not understanding every word that was spoken around me was nothing new. I also knew that encountering new words, in English or any other language, is a rich learning experience.

I know there are versions of Shakespeare's plays adapted for children that do change or modernize Shakespeare's language. I think the assumption is that the only way children can understand the play is if they first encounter the words in modernized English. I never tested that assumption, because I always thought more of my students. Why not let them try the original language; if they have trouble understanding something, we will address this and clarify the words or lines. I never tested that assumption either because I didn't think I should change the language of the man who some say invented modern English. I learned not to underestimate children's ability to understand and even embrace the language of the world's greatest storyteller, even as adults everywhere around the world have done for hundreds of years.

# CONDENSING A PLAY, STEP BY STEP

Following are the steps I go through when I condense a script.

## Read the play and start to condense a script for your group of children

To condense a play, first read it through just for the pleasure of it. I usually get a used paperback of the play to do this, because it's inexpensive and I don't mind writing on the pages. You can also go to a Web site such as www.absoluteshakespeare.com for complete texts of the plays and print one out.

Think about the students who will perform the play and note in the margins the most important and manageable parts for the children who will use the script. At the beginning of this process I make checkmarks in pencil next to scenes I think I will use and question marks by those I don't think I will use. I may also decide to cut or eliminate all or parts of long soliloquies by drawing a diagonal line across them, and do the same for scenes peripheral to the main story line, or with characters I don't think I will use. I also underline any character's lines I know I want to retain, for example, "Out damned spot!" spoken by Lady Macbeth. I continue to go through the play and mark it up this way in pencil, deleting scenes and characters and noting others to keep.

## Follow the main plotline: tell the story

Read the play to find the main plotline. Delete characters, scenes, and subplots that are peripheral to the main plot. For example, in *Macbeth* Hecate is a character who calls herself "the mistress of your charms" in a scene with the three witches. Her character is not necessary, however, for the witches to do the magic and prophesying necessary to tell the story. I cut the parts of the scenes with Hecate by drawing a diagonal line through them, to begin to cut the play down. You can eliminate subplots and associated characters this way, as well as any other scenes you don't feel are necessary to move the story forward. (Having said this about Hecate, see the step below about reviewing the script, in which I discuss adding the character of Hecate back in because of the singing talent of a child in the group).

A good example of cutting both a character and a subplot is in *Romeo and Juliet*. Juliet's father has decided that she will marry Paris. Before this can happen, she has married Romeo. She has scenes with Paris, but they are not necessary to move the plotline forward. Paris can be referred to by Juliet's father, mother, nurse, Friar Laurence, and Juliet, but he doesn't actually have to appear in a scene. On the other hand, if you have an older group of students and want to keep the character of Paris, you could include him, for example, in the exciting scene where he goes to the Capulet tomb after her death and is killed by Romeo in a sword fight.

The bottom line is that you have to cut not only lines but whole scenes to make a manageable script for children. How you do it depends not only on the number and age of students, but keeping the plot moving so the story can be told in 30 to 45 minutes. A staged version of one of Shakespeare's plays with every line and scene used could take two to three hours. When transferred to film, directors make cuts similar to those I've described here. They simply can't film large outdoor crowd or fight scenes and take advantage of being able to carry on a fight all over the streets of Verona, as in *Romeo and Juliet*, and still include every spoken line, in a two-hour film.

# Revise the script during rehearsals as needed

Think of the script as a living, working draft, rather than a final product. The play performance itself is your final product. Things will happen during rehearsals that you can't anticipate, but the good news is that you can continue to adapt your condensed script draft according to the children's ideas, talents, and needs, or unexpected events.

For example, during a summer program with third- to fifth-grade students performing *Macbeth*, we were blocking the play. Blocking is the placement and movement of actors in a dramatic presentation: entrances, exits, where to stand, how to move, learning to face the audience, when and how to say lines, and so on. We hit a snag, however, with the boy playing Macduff. When he had volunteered to be Macduff , he seemed well suited to the part. He was a tall, enthusiastic fifth grader and said he couldn't wait to get his sword. His third-grade brother was in the group as well. He was younger than the other students, but his mother had asked to sign him up anyway because it would be easier for her to have them in the same class during the summer. She added that he was a good kid, mature for his age, and indeed he was. He volunteered to be a soldier in the scenes with Macduff, played by his older brother.

As we blocked the scene, we added dialogue. It was Macduff's big scene with lines. It is the last scene, with the battle between the English army led by Macduff to depose the tyrant Macbeth from the throne of Scotland. The boy playing Macduff confronted Macbeth on the battlefield and was supposed to say, "Turn hellhound, turn!" But he simply could not say the line. His stuttering was acute. He was obviously upset and frustrated. He froze.

Meanwhile, his younger brother was standing next to him. As I wondered how to make this work, the younger brother stepped forward, looked at the script, pointed at Macbeth, and changed the line to "Macduff wants you to turn, hellhound, turn!" We all saw the magic of a child solving a problem, supporting another child, and making the play work. The line was said, and Macduff rushed forward. Macbeth turned, and he and Macduff made a few sword exchanges in slow motion. (I had told them that we would do this at first and then work on carefully blocking the whole fight later in rehearsals.) Macduff killed Macbeth in the inevitable end of the play.

The crowd (the other children and myself) went wild. We cheered and clapped. During our debriefing after the play, I asked the same and only question I ever ask, "What did you see that you liked?" A very mature young Lady Macbeth said, " I liked the way Macduff rushed forward to kill Macbeth while the soldier said Macbeth should turn. He caught Macbeth by surprise. They did a good job." Older brother Macduff and younger brother the soldier both beamed with pride. So we made the subtle change in the line to "My lord Macduff commands you to turn, hell-hound, turn!"

After rehearsal I saw the boys rush up to their mother, talking excitedly. She came up to me and said rather sheepishly that she was afraid that if she had told me the older brother had a speech problem in certain circumstances, I wouldn't have let him join the class. She thanked me for allowing the younger brother to join the class, as he was often able to assist his older brother in this way. I told her, first, that I would never turn a child away, that we would work together to accommodate that child, and second, I didn't underestimate children in their ability to solve problems when they were truly engaged in a learning experience.

The most important thing in condensing a script is to make it work for your students. Whether you do it, or as in this example, they do it themselves, accommodating them rather than strictly adhering to what you included in your original condensed script draft is what is important.

# Review your script for each new group of children

I often did a new script for each new performance, depending on the age level of students, the number of students, and in some cases, any special talents they might have. As I mentioned above, I usually deleted the part of Hecate in the witches' scenes in *Macbeth*. However, one time I added it back when I had a student who was a talented singer. The part includes lines that can be performed as a song. The child and her father, who was himself a singer, researched and found a tune for the words. It was a part of the original play, and it was a way to showcase her special talent.

Reviewing helps me rethink a play. Each time I revise one of my condensed scripts, I find some new insight into the play, and it keeps my perspective and enthusiasm fresh for each new performance. I am also mindful of the group of students who will be performing the play and ask myself how I might differentiate the script for their special talents or needs.

It would indeed be easier if I could say that I have condensed one script for each of the plays that will work with every group of students, but this simply has not been my experience. Luckily, every play by Shakespeare is much longer than you need and a very deep well of ideas, characters, and scenes, so that you can make choices about what to use based on your group of students. I have used the script I condensed for *Macbeth* (see appendix B) many times, but I have also adapted it many times, as when we tweaked lines so that the younger brother of Macduff described previously could say the lines for him. I have also condensed *Macbeth* for older groups, and with changes that reflected the group I was working with, as in adding back in the character Hecate for the girl who could sing.

It has also been my experience that things will happen after you start rehearsals that will require changes, but it is all right to change what you've already changed anyway.

## A Final Word

Don't underestimate children. They will always surprise you.

# CHAPTER 4

# Casting a Play

This chapter describes my method of introducing the play to children and then immediately letting them cast themselves, all in the first session. I include questions they often ask about a character to help them decide which part they would like to play. I also demythologize casting Shakespeare with children with regard to issues such as gender, lead parts, and costuming. Ways to balance the participation so all children are involved are also described.

## INTRODUCE THE PLAY AND LET CHILDREN CAST THEMSELVES

In the first session, I tell students which play we will do and the story of the play, then cast it immediately. We begin to block the first scene within the first hour of beginning. Their job is to start to learn their lines before the next session. The process I use is discussed step by step in the following sections.

### Tell the story of the play

I tell the story of the play to introduce it. See chapter 2 for a narrative of the story of each of the ten plays I have performed with children. You could read the one I've provided for the play you've chosen, or adapt it and tell it in your own words.

Sometimes I use pictures related to the play, such as a photograph of a play production or a drawing of a scene. For many years I used *A Shakespeare Coloring Book* (1989), which I bought at a museum. The cover shows a vintage illustration of Shakespeare with a piece of paper and a quill pen, and the first page shows a vintage illustration, "The Great Globe itself." The rest of the book shows vintage black-and-white illustrations and notes that, "Shakespearean pictures to color were very popular early in the 19th century. These sold for a Penny Plain, Tuppence Colored, and they adorned many an English nursery." See appendix A for sources of other images you could use.

You could also use props to tell the story, such as a costume item or a prop you would use in the play. Use your imagination and make it engaging. I have found that once I tell students we will perform the play, they hang on every word as I tell about it.

## Pass out the condensed scripts

I next give each child a copy of the script I have condensed. The cover sheet has the name of the play and a list of the cast of characters on it. I go down the list and say a few words about each of the characters, then give the children a few minutes to look over the list and think about which part they would like to play if they could choose. I also tell them to think about more than one part so they can be flexible when we cast the play. After that I ask if they have any questions that would help them decide which part or parts they want to play. Children typically ask the following questions:

❖ How many lines does the character have?

❖ Do I get a sword?

❖ Do I get to use it?

❖ Do I get to die?

❖ Do I kill anyone?

❖ Do I get to be funny?

❖ What do I wear?

After answering their questions briefly, I give them some more time to think. Over the years I have learned to be ready to tell them about the size of a part: how many lines the character has and how many scenes he or she appears in. I note this next to each character on my script. Some children have a very definite idea about the size of the part they would like to play. Some want a small part or medium part; others want a large part. It all depends on the child.

## Take volunteers for the parts

When the children seem to have an idea about the parts they would like to play, I explain the procedure we will use to assign them.

First, they will put their heads down as I read the name of each character on the list. When I read a part someone wants, he or she raises a hand. If only one student raises a hand, the part is given to that person, and I write his or her name next to the character's name on my script.

When I've gone through all the characters' names, the children raise their heads, and I tell them which parts have been cast. (A part is cast only if only one child raised a hand for it.) I tell them which parts have been cast and with whom, which parts have more than one volunteer and will have to be resolved, and which parts remain uncast. Many of the parts are cast the first time we do this.

## What to do if more than one child wants a part

If more than one child wants a part, we negotiate. I give them a chance to pick one of the remaining parts and answer any more questions they may have. Most of them are eager to have a part even if it is their second choice and will volunteer for it as this point.

If more than one child still wants the same part, I suggest some lines they can look over and then read to the rest of the class. I let them take a few minutes to do this while I take questions from children who already have a part. When they seem ready, each child who wants the part reads the same lines. Everyone lowers their heads again, and the class votes secretly for the person they feel should have the part.

# WHY LET CHILDREN CAST THEMSELVES?

I thought a lot about how to do this the first time I did Shakespeare with children. I felt it would not be a meaningful experience for students unless they truly had a hand in producing the play from the beginning by casting it themselves. I wanted this experience to be student centered and equitable and give every child a chance to go for the part he or she really wanted to play. I also didn't want to assume that I knew which child was best for which part. I believed my students could be the best judge of that. Nor did I want a child's parents deciding which part was best, which is why I introduced the play, cast it, and started rehearsing in the first session.

I wanted to be careful not to assume that the "best" readers or writers or best-behaved students should automatically take the leads in these plays. I based this decision on my own experience as one of the "best readers, writers, and teacher's pets," who was often cast in the lead of a play or as a narrator simply because I was good at reading and at paper and pencil tasks. I was shy about performing and did not enjoy being on a stage.

When I shared this concern with one of my Shakespeare parents one time, saying that I wasn't sure why I liked performing Shakespeare with children so much when I had never had any desire to act or be on a stage, she said, "Carole, you're a director!" I also remember school plays in high school in which the leads were often played wonderfully by students who did not excel in the traditional academic classes that I did. I saw drama as a means to offer the non- "paper and pencil kids" a chance to excel and be engaged in another way of learning.

This procedure worked, although not always for the reasons I thought it would. I am really happy that I gave every child a chance to pick a part. I learned very quickly that children invariably want to play the part they feel they are most suited for and that is within their capabilities. They all want to do their best, help the play production succeed, and enjoy it. Letting them self-select virtually guarantees this. I also learned that when children take responsibility for casting themselves, and often negotiating which part they will play, they develop a greater tolerance for sharing and cooperating, and they learn the real meaning of teamwork. I was honestly amazed at how quickly they were able to do this and how happy they were with whatever part they had, even if it wasn't their first choice.

Gradually I realized that it is adults who have so many preconceived ideas about Shakespeare, including certain roles. Children haven't learned these biases yet. They just know they are going to have fun doing a play. Only once did a student seem disgruntled when another student was chosen to be Juliet in *Romeo and Juliet*. She had already played Juliet in my summer program when she was younger, and I think she assumed she would play it again. This was a group of middle school students, and I am pretty sure that almost every girl in the group had noticed the boy who looked like he would volunteer to play Romeo (he did). When the two girls read for the part the group did not choose the Juliet veteran, and she was obviously unhappy. She sulked a little, and by the time she was willing to participate in the casting, the only part left was that of Lord Capulet, Juliet's father. She was not pleased, but the only other option would have been to leave the group. The other girl was a wonderful Juliet and a great team player. She seemed to make an extra effort with her former rival for the part, and by the end of the production they were great friends.

Deciding to introduce the play and cast it in one session with no prior fanfare kept the focus on my students. They decided, literally, what parts they would play based on their own interests and knowledge of their abilities , not those of the teacher or a parent. It gave them both a choice and responsibility for their decisions, something that is crucial throughout any play production. You want children to learn to make good choices and take responsibility for their own actions. Starting out that way in the first session sets the tone for the rest of the experience.

What I remember most about doing *Macbeth* in fourth grade was that there were "two" Lady Macbeths and that I was first going to be the "crazy" one and then changed to the "evil" one. I think that really helped me see that the character developed and changed and that she felt the consequences of her actions. It might have been my first real lesson in ethics and how our destructive side can turn back on us and end up destroying us. I liked the feeling of the power of the "evil" Lady Macbeth, but felt the "crazy" one's role (played by Martha Askins, my best friend) had more dramatic interest for the audience.

Felicia Roberts, in Carole Cox's fourth/fifth-grade class,
Shorewood Hills Elementary, Madison, Wisconsin, 1968–1969

What I don't remember about doing Shakespeare in your class, because I think it didn't happen, was any angst about learning lines or making costumes or competing for parts. Perhaps others recall things differently, but I have no recollection of hurt feelings or jealousies at work. It all seemed like play and story telling.

Martha Askins, in Carole Cox's fourth/fifth-grade class,
Shorewood Hills Elementary, Madison, Wisconsin, 1968–1969

# DEMYTHOLOGIZING CASTING SHAKESPEARE WITH CHILDREN

I have learned to demythologize many of the preconceptions I had, or things I worried about that simply didn't happen when casting a play with children. Other things that happened were pleasant surprises. I describe these here because they are often questions I'm asked by teachers, librarians, and others who might do Shakespeare with children. There are plenty of things to worry about, without including things that I just haven't found to be a problem.

## Disregard gender

No distinction according to gender need be made when casting Shakespeare. Girls will have to play male parts, for the obvious reason that is there are many more male parts than female parts in his plays. I have never found this to be a problem. Children pick a part because the character interests them. They seem to intuitively understand that it is not about whether characters are male or female but who they are and what they do or even what motivates them.

Some of my best Hamlets have been wonderfully intense girls, and Lady Macbeth was once a perfectly ruthless fourth-grade boy. Supernatural creatures such as witches, fairies, ghosts, and monsters are always open to both genders. Somehow this genderless casting works with Shakespeare. During Shakespeare's time all parts, including female parts, were played by males. His many supernatural characters seem genderless. Is Ariel or Caliban in *The Tempest* or Puck in *A Midsummer Night's Dream* definitively male or female? It's hard to tell, and what difference does it make anyway? Another factor is that in the middle and upper elementary grades and even through middle school, girls may be taller and bigger than many boys. Except for dress and hair, boys and girls at these ages often appear remarkably similar when they are in costume.

With appropriate costuming, audiences are not always sure whether or not it is a girl or a boy playing a part. One summer I had an all-girl cast for *Romeo and Juliet*. It just happened that way. The girl playing Romeo was a natural actor and shorter than the girl who played Juliet. We staged the play to hide the height difference: Juliet always sat down when Romeo was in the scene, was on the balcony, or was dead. One audience member commented to me afterward, "That little guy playing Romeo was terrific." I told the little girl who had played Romeo, and she was very proud.

Shakespeare also used gender disguise in *Twelfth Night*, one of the plays I recommend for children, especially upper elementary and middle school students. A young woman disguises herself as a young man throughout most of the play. Even if I wasn't doing *Twelfth Night* with children, I always had a Shakespeare library in the room with paperback copies of the plays; collections of stories of the plays; and other books about Shakespeare, the Renaissance, and stagecraft. (See appendix A.) I often did booktalks about other plays or referred students to books containing information about things that were happening during our production of a play. For example if girls were playing boys' parts, I would refer them to *Twelfth Night*.

## Girls like to play Hamlet and soldiers

Although I have had a few girls whose first question about a character during the discussion during that first casting session was, "Does the character wear a dress?", they are far outweighed by the girls who raised their hands for the role of Hamlet, Brutus or Mark Antony in *Julius Caesar*, any of the young rakes in *Romeo and Juliet* (such as Benvolio, Tybalt, or Mercutio), and soldiers in *Macbeth* or *Julius Caesar*.

One of the great benefits of drama is that children in roles can put themselves into another's place and try it on for size. It's the same reason we encourage reading literature as a way of knowing about other people, other parts of the world, or other times. Pretending to be someone quite different from oneself allows students to explore and learn about that character and indeed, about themselves. Not to mention the fact that children like to pretend, and do so frequently, freely, and openly. This willingness and interest in being someone else, someone even very different, was revealed to me when girls continually raised their hands to be Hamlet or a warrior.

Over the years I have had girls play many male parts, including the lead in *Hamlet,* Mark Antony in *Julius Caesar*, Romeo in *Romeo and Juliet*, Theseus and Oberon in *A Midsummer Night's Dream*, and Prospero in *The Tempest*, as well as almost every other type of male part in the Shakespeare plays that I have done with children.

## Boys like the way they look in tights

Adults such as teachers and librarians who are attending presentations I have made at educational conferences on doing Shakespeare with children, or parents, often ask me how I talked boys into wearing tights. First, let me point out that you can costume a play any way you want; I like simple costuming. I think *Julius Caesar* is best done when children wear light-colored shorts, a white T-shirt, a towel, or an old cut up white sheet for a toga, and sandals. You can throw a purple piece of cloth over Caesar's shoulder and offer him a crown of fake leaves, but that is all you need. Furthermore, a Renaissance play can be done without tights. Children can wear all black, or dark sweatpants or shorts and big belted shirts over them, for example, and you can throw in a cape or a hat for interest.

However, in my experience doing Renaissance-setting plays like *Romeo and Juliet, The Taming of the Shrew*, or *Twelfth Night,* boys who wear a costume with tights, such as most of the young men in the play would wear, really like the way they look in tights. I once had a boy in *Romeo and*

*Juliet* who cried when he fell and got a run in his beautiful peacock blue tights. His mother got new ones and a spare pair in case it happened again. I go into more detail about costuming in chapter 6, but if you do go with the Renaissance style with tights, you can add a pair of shorts with a casing on the legs for elastic so you have the puffy look of Sir Walter Raleigh over the tights. I always give children the option of wearing the shorts. Sometimes they decline, and then they have to wear dark—not white, which can easily be dyed dark—underwear underneath. When boys went for the "tights only" option, I often saw them looking over their shoulders to check out how they looked in their tights. Boys like the way they look in tights.

## The big parts are not always preferred

The first play I did with children was *Hamlet*, and I was worried that too many children would want to play the lead. To my surprise, we had to coax one of the students into playing it. When I asked my students about their lack of interest in playing Hamlet, one commented, "Too many lines. He's weird."

The most popular part that first time was the Ghost. I think I had five hands go up to play the Ghost of Hamlet's father. These were fourth- and fifth-grade students, and I later realized, why wouldn't they rather be a Ghost than a tortured, confused young man who is riddled with doubt? The same thing happened the first time I did *Macbeth*. The most popular parts were the Witches and Banquo. Children were very interested in the scene when Banquo's Ghost appears in bloody rags and chains. Why wouldn't they rather play a bloody, chain-rattling ghost than a tortured, confused older man who is riddled with doubt? Or powerful witches who make prophesies and potions, sing chants, and dance around a cauldron? It began to make sense to me. These were children, not actors looking to make a reputation on the legitimate stage. These were my fourth- and fifth-grade students. I watched them many times chase each other around in the yard pretending to be Spiderman. Why wouldn't they want to play a supernatural character or a character with super powers?

The big idea here is that the big parts are not always preferred. Children are most interested in what the character does. Some don't want to learn all the lines required of a lead and will tell you that. Students who repeated my summer program would often specifically ask how many lines the character had. At first I thought it was not important, but I could see they were in earnest. I started telling them whether a part was small, medium, or large and how many lines there were in each size. They will also ask how many scenes a character is in. I think some of them just love moving on and off stage.

# BALANCING CHILDREN AND PARTS

I address this topic in chapter 3 also, but even after you have condensed and prepared the script, and children have volunteered for the parts, you may need to negotiate with them things like splitting big parts, sharing lines, or combining small parts during the casting process.

## Split parts

If you are doing a play with an upper elementary grade class of 30 children or more, it's likely that you will have more children than you have parts for them to play with a ratio of one part per child. If so, you can split large parts. This means that two different children play one of the larger parts. They share a costume. You would just have to decide how to divide the scenes between them.

For example, you can split the parts of Macbeth and Lady Macbeth so that four children play this power couple. Macbeth splits nicely before and after the murder of King Duncan, and Lady Macbeth can be split before and after she goes mad. I am always amazed that this technique is so little noticed by the audience. When students wear the same costume, and you play down any distinguishing features such as hair with a hat or hood, the change is not that noticeable. I have even had both a boy and a girl split a part. I remember one time remarking to a parent how well this technique had worked, and she argued with me, saying that it must have been the same child playing the part. The children were pleased when I told them.

In *Macbeth* you can also split the three witches. In a short version of the play, as in appendix B, the witches appear in two scenes. They can also appear in the background of the last battle scene, without lines. Cast six children to play the three witches, three in one scene and three in another. Splitting or double casting these parts would give you two Macbeths, two Lady Macbeths, and six witches, or ten children in a class of thirty for just three parts.

In *Romeo and Juliet* you could split Romeo and Juliet and Friar Laurence, as they all appear in several scenes. In *Hamlet*, Hamlet and his mother Gertrude could be split. In *Julius Caesar*, Mark Antony could be split, with one child speaking the "Friends, Romans, and countrymen scene" and another child in all the other scenes. In *The Taming of the Shrew*, two children could play Petruchio, and two could play Kate. Prospero in *The Tempest* and the lead in *Richard the III* could be split. In *Twelfth Night*, you could split the Duke, Olivia, and Viola/Cesario.

## *Parts to Split in Ten Plays*

1. *Macbeth*: Macbeth, Lady Macbeth, the three Witches

2. *Hamlet*: Hamlet, Gertrude, Claudius

3. *Romeo and Juliet*: Romeo, Juliet, Friar Laurence

4. *Julius Caesar*: Brutus, Mark Antony

5. *A Midsummer Night's Dream*: Oberon, Titania, Puck

6. *The Comedy of Errors*: Antipholuses and Dromios of Ephesus and Syracuse—already split; two sets of twins

7. *The Taming of the Shrew*: Katarina, Petruchio, Grumio

8. *Twelfth Night*: Orsino, Olivia, Viola

9. *The Tempest*: Prospero, Ariel

10. *Richard III*: Richard

# Parts that can share lines

Several children may share lines of characters that are similar in a scene. They would all appear in the scene but share the lines and take turns speaking, to achieve a balance. Or lines from a character you are not using but who is in the original scene could be given to a character you have included in the condensed version of the scene (e.g., the conspirators in *Julius Caesar*). This works well with parts that are more generic, such as A Murderer (make it more), A Gravedigger (how about two?), or A Fairy (any number can play), and all can share.

## *Parts to Share Lines in Ten Plays*

1. *Macbeth*: Murderers, Noblemen of Scotland, Witches, Soldiers

2. *Hamlet*: Courtiers—Rosencrantz, Guildenstern, Osric; Officers/Soldiers—Marcellus, Barnardo, Francisco; Gravediggers, Players

3. *Romeo and Juliet*: Servants to Montague—Balthasar, Abram; Servants to Capulet—Sampson, Gregory, Peter

4. *Julius Caesar*: Conspirators against Julius Caesar—Marcus Brutus, Cassius, Casca, Trebonius, Ligarius, Decius Brutus, Metellus Cimber; Tribunes—Flavius, Marullus

5. *A Midsummer Night's Dream*: Peaseblossom, Cobweb, Mote, Mustardseed—fairies, and Other Fairies

6. *The Comedy of Errors*: A Merchant and Another Merchant, Jailer, Headsman, Officers and Other Attendants

7. *The Taming of the Shrew*: Servants to Lucentio—Tranio, Biondello; Servants to Petruchio, Grumio, Curtis, Nathaniel, Phillip, Joseph, Nicholas, Peter

8. *Twelfth Night*: Antonio a Sea Captain, friend to Sebastian and A Sea Captain, friend to Viola; Gentleman attending on the Duke—Valentine, Curio; Servants to Olivia—Fabian, Feste, a clown

9. *The Tempest*: Lords—Adrian, Francisco; Stephano and Trinculo; Master of a Ship, Boatswain, and Mariners; Spirits—Juno, Ceres, Iris, Nymphs, Reapers and Other Spirits attending on Prospero

10. *Richard III*: Any of the Lords and Ghosts of Richard's victims

Following is an example of how I edited a scene from *A Midsummer Night's Dream,* condensing the lines that the main characters Titania and Oberon speak, and having The Fairies share lines in a song to balance the parts. Even though Shakespeare called them The Fairies, I gave each one a number and a fairy name Shakespeare used elsewhere in the play, so the children playing these parts could feel that these were their special lines and they had special names. I didn't change the language or the order of the lines. I deleted some for Titania and Oberon, and had The Fairies—now named Fairy 1, Peaseblossom; Fairy 2, Cobweb; and Fairy 3, Moth—share lines in a song where Shakespeare had the instruction, "The Fairies sing." I indicated All Fairies where they say the lines together in one section.

The whole passage is shown on pages 47–48, but the boldface lines are those I retained, showing how I split the parts for Fairy 1, 2, and 3. I adapted the list of characters to look like this:

Titania, Queen of the Fairies

Oberon, King of the Fairies

Fairy 1, Peaseblossom

Fairy 2, Cobweb

Fairy 3, Moth

# Scene II

*[Another part of the wood. Enter Titania with her train.]*

**Titania:** **Come now a roundel and a fairy song.**

Then for the third part of a minute, hence;

Some to kill cankers in the musk-rose buds,

Some war with rere-mice for their leathern wings,

To make my small elves coats, and some keep back

The clamorous owl that nightly hoots and wonders

At our quaint spirits.

**Sing me now asleep;**

Then to your offices **and let me rest.**

*[The Fairies sing.]*

**Fairy 1:** **You spotted snakes with double tongue,**

**Thorny hedgehogs, be not seen;**

**Newts and blind-worms, do no wrong,**

**Come not near our fairy queen.**

**All Fairies:** **Philomel, with melody**

**Sing in our sweet lullaby;**

**Lulla, lulla, lullaby, lulla, lulla, lullaby:**

**Never harm,**

**nor spell nor charm**

**Come our lovely lady nigh;**

**So, good night, with lullaby.**

**Fairy 2:** **Weaving spiders, come not here;**

**Hence, you long-legg'd spinners, hence!**

**Beetles black, approach not near;**

**Worm nor snail, do no offence.**

Philomel, with melody, &c.

*[A Fairy.]*

From *Shakespeare Kids: Performing his Plays, Speaking his Words* by Carole Cox. Santa Barbara, CA: Libraries Unlimited. Copyright © 2010.

**Fairy 3:** **Hence, away!**

**Now all is well:**

**One aloof stand sentinel.**

[*Exit Fairies. Titania sleeps. Enter Oberon and squeezes the flower onto Titania's eyelids.*]

**Oberon:** **What thou seest when thou dost wake,**

**Do it for thy true-love take**

Love and languish for his sake:

Be it ounce, or cat, or bear,

Pard, or boar with bristled hair,

In thy eye that shall appear

When thou wakest, it is thy dear:

Wake when some vile thing is near.

[*Exit.*]

From *Shakespeare Kids: Performing his Plays, Speaking his Words* by Carole Cox. Santa Barbara, CA: Libraries Unlimited. Copyright © 2010.

Three children share the fairy song, each with his or her own lines, but also sharing a portion and singing it together.

# Combine small parts

If you have fewer children than parts, or want to balance parts so that all children can fully participate, you can combine small parts so that a child can play more than one part. For example, in *Macbeth* the Murderers appear briefly in one scene, where Macbeth tells them to kill Banquo and his son Fleance, followed by the scene where they kill Banquo. They make brief appearances in these two back to back scenes in the middle of the play, so they can also play soldiers in the armies of the English and Scottish forces in the last battle scene. Similarly, the gravediggers in *Hamlet* can also appear as the traveling Players in the "play within the play." In *Julius Caesar*, the conspirators who assassinate Caesar may reappear as members of the Roman mob. By combining parts in this way, you can either make sure every part has a child playing it, or children with smaller parts appear as different characters to balance their participation with children playing larger roles.

## *Small Parts to Combine in Ten Plays*

1. *Macbeth*: Fleance, Siward, Doctor, Porter, Murderers, Gentlewoman; any small part and the part of soldier in the last battle scene.

2. *Hamlet*: Courtiers, Officers, Players, Gravediggers, Lords and Ladies; any small part in the scene to watch the fencing match between Laertes and Hamlet at the end of the play

3. *Romeo and Juliet*: Apothecary, any of the Servants, Lady Montague; any small part in the scene at the Capulet's ball and the final scene when the Duke speaks as a Citizen of Verona

4. *Julius Caesar*: Any of the Conspirators, Senators, friends to Brutus and Cassius, servants, and Citizens, Guards, and Attendants; any small part in the Roman mob that listens to Mark Antony's funeral oration over Caesar's body

5. *A Midsummer Night's Dream*: Philostrate, Egeus, Fairies; any small part attending the play put on by the workmen for the wedding scene

6. *The Comedy of Errors*: Angelo, Merchants, Jailer, Headsman, Officers: any small part in the crowd in the last scene

7. *The Taming of the Shrew*: any of the Servants, the Merchant, Widow, Tailor, Haberdasher, Officer; any small part at Bianca's wedding to Lucentio, the last scene

8. *Twelfth Night*: Antonio, A Sea Captain, Valentine, Curio, Fabian, Feste, Lords, a Priest, Sailors, Officers, Musicians, and Attendants

9. *The Tempest*: Adrian, Francisco, Master of a Ship, Boatswain, Mariners, and Spirits

10. *Richard III*: Any of the smaller parts for Lords or Sirs, children, Ghosts of Richard's victims, Attendants, Bishop, Priest, Sheriff, Keeper, Two Murderers, Page, Citizens, Messengers; all small parts joining in as Soldiers in the last battle scene

In my experience, children enjoy playing more than one role. Roles like Murderers are always popular, and everyone wants to be in the last act of *Macbeth* with a sword, fighting to the death. I always make the offer to the child or children who play Lady Macbeth, even though she's dead by that time, to don a warriors costume, grab a sword and fight in this scene. I've seen a sense of pride develop in children when they knew they were responsible for more than one character, including costume changes; learning lines for more than one character; working with different children in various scenes; and appearing in multiple scenes with cues, entrances, and exits to learn.

# REFERENCES

*A Shakespeare Coloring Book.* 1989. Santa Barbara, CA: Bellerophon Books.

## A Final Word

Trust children's judgment when they cast themselves. They want the play to be good.

# CHAPTER 5

# Rehearsing a Play

This chapter describes practical strategies for learning lines once the play has been cast; staging, blocking, and rehearsing scenes in the classroom and outdoors; revising a script as you rehearse if necessary; and scheduling time for rehearsals in a classroom or a summer or after-school program.

## LEARNING LINES

Once the play has been introduced and cast during the first session, children begin to learn lines. The first time I did Shakespeare with my fourth/fifth grade combination class, I worried that it would be difficult for children to memorize their lines. It was, after all, *Hamlet*. As with many other common myths adults have about children doing Shakespeare, I found out I was wrong. The minute we finished that first session, I saw them marking up their scripts to underline the words they would say. I saw them reading and asking other students or me for words if they needed to. They came to me with questions. The scripts were on their desks all day; they took them out to the playground at recess and lunch and home that night. From this first class to many others, here is what I learned from children about learning lines.

### Learning lines is not a big problem

To my absolute surprise and delight, that first time a few students came in the next morning and told me they had learned all their lines. I'll admit that when I asked if they wanted to share, they did sound a bit like robots, but they knew the lines, and I knew they would be less robotic when we rehearsed a scene in which they would be speaking to another character.

I noticed the keen interest of other students when this happened. I thought I saw a competitive glint in several of their eyes, and the race was on. If Laertes knew his lines, then Polonius, Ophelia, and Hamlet had better learn their lines. Not to be outdone, Polonius, Ophelia, and Hamlet got busy. They asked if they could get in a group for their scenes to practice during group work time if they had finished what they needed to do. I saw them practicing on the playground. Parents told me students asked for help in arranging to meet after school to practice if that was possible, and that they practiced over the phone at home.

The scripts became tattered, often rolled up and occasionally used as props in a pretend sword fight. First and last pages sometimes detached and were lost, so I learned to keep spares on hand. The scripts were visibly present in the room: on desks, the floor, and work tables, and sticking out of desks, backpacks, and back pockets. I thought this was wonderful. My students' favorite possession at that time was their Shakespeare script. I could not have scripted that myself.

## Children haven't yet learned that Shakespeare is supposed to be hard

Why was I surprised that children were eagerly, and often quickly, learning their lines, not to mention the lines of other students? Like many adults, I thought Shakespeare was supposed to be hard, and it would be difficult for students to memorize lines. Obviously my students had not gotten the memo about this. I realized that children, unlike many adults, were unencumbered by a past with Shakespeare. They had not yet learned to think that Shakespeare was "hard."

Committing the language to memory was a great discipline to learn at an early age. It accelerated my appreciation for what Shakespeare could do with language and meter, and predisposed me to savor his genius throughout my life. It also predisposed me to savor the wonders of language in general, of the thoughts and feelings, the history and comedy and tragedy, that might be expressed when words are assembled into the poetry of speech and text.

David Medaris, in Carole Cox's fourth/fifth-grade class at Shorewood Hills Elementary, 1968–1969, and "Shakespeare for Kids" summer programs, Madison, Wisconsin, 1971, 1972, and 1973

One thing to watch out for, in fact, is when children have learned all the lines in the scenes they are in, not just their own lines. I have seen students mouth the lines of other characters, often facing the audience. I'm not sure why this happens, but it does. We talk about it and practice always looking at the character who is talking, keeping our own mouths shut at that time.

## Children identify with the characters, so the lines are meaningful when they speak them

I had also underestimated the identification children felt with their characters. They wanted to learn lines so they could speak as their characters. In fact, lines from Shakespeare were spoken throughout the day. They often began calling each other by their characters' names. During the time we were rehearsing that first *Hamlet*, I asked a child to "get the lights" after we watched a film. He jumped from his seat, struck a pose like a super hero about to fly or a ballet dancer about to leap, and shouted the line that Claudius says after Hamlet has exposed his treachery with the "play within the play": "Give me some light. Away!" He stayed in his super hero/ballet dancer character, flew to the lights, and with a grand gesture, flicked them on.

We were all a little stunned by this little performance, but after a moment, spontaneous applause and laughter broke out. I realized that Shakespeare's wonderful language was living in our classroom, not proving to be a barrier. These occurrences continued. Any time I did *Macbeth* and any child spilled something, he or she seemed compelled to shout, "Out damned spot. Out I say." After all, who wouldn't want to say "damned" in school?

## Children are engaged with the play

I had underestimated the engagement children felt with the whole play. This wasn't something new in my class, but the electricity generated by doing Shakespeare had a higher than usual voltage and rippled across the class. Because they were in scenes with other children, they depended on each other to learn lines as cues for other students. Each child wanted to make the scene work and took responsibility for learning his or her own lines. I sat back a minute and marveled at their enthusiasm and earnest work, and thought about why this was happening.

I realized that this is not just rote memorization, as in learning a poem to recite. The lines are connected to actions and conversation with another character. As students identified with their characters, the lines were the way they expressed themselves as those characters. The lines were meaningful. The children had things to do in a scene and things to say to other characters. This was how the story is told in a play.

## Set a "drop scripts" day and stick to it

As the rehearsals progress, and you see that a majority of students have learned their lines, set a day to "drop scripts"—having no scripts in hand when the children rehearse. Then stick to it. Some students may already be rehearsing without their scripts, but you can't wait until the last child doesn't seem to need a script to set a deadline. This can be a big day for the whole group. It takes them a big step closer to the performance.

There are several things I do after the "drop scripts" day. I stick to the date and don't allow any scripts in a scene rehearsal. The students who have already learned their lines are fine with this. Those who have not can look at their lines right before they enter a scene. I prompt them for a few more rehearsals, but I also tell them when I'm going to stop. At that point, I explain that prompting by myself or even other students sends a signal to the audience that they are not really the characters because someone else has to tell them what to say. If they forget a line, they should make up something similar to what the character needs to say, conveying the meaning of the words if not the exact words. If they still can't think of their lines, then the other characters have to pick up the story and carry it forward by improvising as well.

I have seen a child go blank in a scene, and another student will say, "Do you mean to tell me that . . . ," paraphrasing what the other student would have said. Students learn to support and rely on each other and think on their feet. I have too much respect for them and their abilities to jump in and rescue them. In my experience, they do a great job of saving themselves, each other, and the scene. It's a great learning experience, and the show must go on.

## "Arise Sir or Lady . . ." (who has learned all his or her lines)

Once, during that first *Hamlet* we did, on a whim I decided to honor the first child who had learned all his or her lines. We had stage foils for the fight between Hamlet and Laertes, so I grabbed one and started to act like the Queen knighting a person. I told the child to kneel, then tapped him or her on each shoulder as I said something like,

> For executing faithfully your duty in learning all your lines and speaking them without a script in the play *Hamlet*, as your Queen and sovereign lady, I do hereby bestow upon you the station of knight [or lady] of the realm. Arise Sir or Lady [child's name].

Although I was feeling silly, the children seemed enchanted. One asked if everybody got to be knighted if they learned their lines. I told them that since I was the Queen, I could do it whenever I wanted. Since that time, every child has looked forward to this simple little teacher improvisation that says to them that they did a great job—and the Queen is well pleased.

# STAGING THE PLAY

I have done Shakespeare with children in the classroom during the school year, outside during the summer on school playgrounds and on university campuses, and in the front or back yards of private homes. I once directed a Shakespeare Club at a middle school, but that was the only time I have performed Shakespeare with children on an auditorium stage. They were eighth-grade students, better able to handle projecting their voices and becoming a presence on the stage. That was really the only place we could perform, and I always rehearse in the same place we will perform.

## Stage, block, and rehearse scenes in the same place you will perform the play

I have always staged and rehearsed plays where they will be performed. I think children need to be in the same environment all the way through the production of the play. The only time I moved a production, the problems that ensued confirmed my usual approach of staying in one place. I was doing a summer program at Louisiana State University as part of a graduate education class in the arts and elementary education. I met with the teachers who were enrolled in the early morning for the graduate class, they observed me going through all the steps of doing a play immediately afterward, and then they did case studies on the children.

I staged *Romeo and Juliet* against the backdrop of the education building, which was conveniently a Renaissance style. There was a small, raised concrete area with steps we used as a stage, and I pitched a small tent with colorful banners next to it for children to enter when they were not in a scene. The audience sat on the grass. When we rehearsed, the teachers in my graduate class were our practice audience.

After our final performance, one of the teachers asked if we could perform the play at her church for the children in their summer child-care programs. She said she would help. I agreed, with some misgivings. We tried moving the production to the large main church area, using the space in front of the altar as a stage. It was difficult for me to coordinate enough time for rehearsals, between the children's schedules and the availability of the room. We had to talk through many of the adaptations rather than really practice in the space, and the result was that my students were sometimes disoriented, scooting through pews to get on and off stage because they'd made a wrong turn somewhere, missing cues because they were too far away and couldn't hear, and so on. We got through it, but we didn't feel great about it. This confirmed my belief that you just can't go on the road with children, especially younger elementary students. It's best if students stage, block, rehearse, and perform in the same, familiar setting.

## Avoid stages

I had already decided to avoid stages before the first time I did Shakespeare with children. My class had written a musical based on Ian Fleming's book *Chitty Chitty Bang Bang* (before the Disney movie). They wrote the script in five acts, with songs and dance choreographies for each act. They had made a large cardboard car with the same name as the title of the book. Our play was "Chitty

Chitty Bang Bang Around the World." Each act was set in a different country that we had studied in social studies.

Our school had a wonderful old stage in the gym where folding chairs could be set up for audiences. The custodian used the stage for storage of extra furniture, and I was the only teacher who wanted to use it to perform a play. I had many discussions with the principal and the custodian about moving the furniture, and we all agreed on a schedule. That was the plan, but that was not what happened.

Several times we trooped upstairs from our below-ground-level room to the auditorium in our costumes, hauling the student-made car and other props, only to find that the custodian had not moved the furniture or said our rehearsal wasn't on his schedule. The furniture was finally moved and the schedule resolved, but the next time we tried to rehearse, the speech teacher had seen the now empty stage and was there with a group of children. She said now that the stage was clear, she would use it for her classes.

We finally performed "Chitty," but I told myself I would not try to use the stage again. It wasn't just the problem of getting rehearsal time; it was difficult to manage the group with children behind curtains on both sides of a huge stage and me in front it. The main problem, however, was that it was too hard to hear most of the children, not just the very soft-spoken ones. I was constantly saying "Louder!" standing right in front of the stage. I knew this would be an even bigger problem when the chairs were set up for the audience even further away.

When I later did *Hamlet* that first time at the same school, we moved to an open multipurpose room nearer our classroom, which actually had a small, raised, wooden portable platform that we could use as a stage. The room was used by a special resource teacher who provided an enrichment program several days a week at our school and was at other schools on other days. She was also a good friend. I scheduled the use of the room with her successfully, but we still had to move to the room. We also had to set up chairs for the audience and do several performances because there wasn't much room for folding chairs.

I finally got it: I would figure out a way to stay in our own room. The children were at home there, we only had to move our own furniture around, we didn't have to move props, and children who weren't in a scene could continue with other work during rehearsals. The best thing was that I could schedule rehearsals any time.

# Staging Shakespeare in the classroom

## *Room and Furniture Arrangement: Entrances and Exits*

I like to stage Shakespeare in the round in the classroom. This requires pushing back the desks from the center of the room to form a large circle for the audience and leaving some spaces between desks at intervals for the players to enter and exit. Additional audience members may stand in the back of the room. You can also do multiple performances to accommodate more people. Other classes can come to your room and watch the play.

You need an entrance and an exit to the room for the players as well. My room had one door, and when we started to rehearse, we used it as both the entrance and the exit. This was not ideal. We were doing *Macbeth*, and there were moments when it seemed like characters were passing each other coming on and off stage even though they would have been going in opposite directions in the story. The other problem was that anyone not in the scene had to be out in the hall; as good as they were, they were children and it was tempting to move around and talk while others were rehearsing a scene. If you have two doors in a room, entrances and exits are easier, but you still have some children out in the hall together when not onstage.

## *Using a Flat*

The solution was a "flat," which served as a screen in front of the room opposite the classroom door in the back of the room. I found a rolling chalkboard no one was using, and we attached large pieces of cardboard to the front of it. Then we used butcher paper and more cardboard and paint to create a great Scottish castle on the front. We put wooden blocks under the wheels so it wouldn't roll around during the play. When not using the flat, we removed the blocks and rolled it out of the way.

Now we had not only the classroom door but each side of the castle as entrances and exits. Some students could be behind the castle flat and some in the hall. We also used the spaces between desks to enter and exit behind the castle flat or the hall. This worked and became the system I used many times.

## *Materials for a Flat*

There are several simple ways to make a flat:

❖ Stretch a rope or wire between two walls and attach a backdrop to it (e.g., butcher paper or a sheet or fabric may be painted with fabric paints). Use plastic clothes pins or clips to attach the backdrop to the wire or rope. Move the backdrop aside when you don't need it.

❖ Use a rolling chalk or white board, securing it so that the board doesn't move.

❖ Use a simple folding screen.

❖ Decorate a flat with pieces of fabric to create a simple drape (e.g., red and blue for a Renaissance look, purple for *Julius Caesar*, or net and sparkly material for *A Midsummer Night's Dream*).

**Performing *Macbeth* in classroom with raised platform and cloth flat**

## *Other Ways to Use the Classroom*

Lights may be turned on and off to signal a change of scene or mood, and may even be left off if you want to use a spotlight, flashlights, or lanterns with batteries. If you have windows, pull your shades and use lights for the dark moods in *Hamlet, Macbeth,* or *Julius Caesar.* If you have windows that have trees and nature showing through, leave them open for plays like *A Midsummer Night's Dream* or *The Tempest.* You can create some very interesting special effects with very simple lighting.

Student art depicting scenes from the play could also decorate the whole room. Make large posters advertising the play and put them on the door or a bulletin board in the hall.

The advantages of staging in the classroom are that you don't have to move, you won't have scheduling conflicts, and the audience is very close to the young players so they can hear and see everything.

# Staging Shakespeare outdoors

When I started doing a summer program by popular demand from parents of children in other classes in my school as well as my own students, who wanted to do more Shakespeare, I arranged to teach it as a class in the city's recreation program in Madison, Wisconsin. I thought I might be able to do it in my own classroom, but there were too many problems with insurance and custodial help. I was left doing it on the playground, which turned out to be a lucky change.

## *Outdoor Flats*

I knew I needed a flat for an entrance and an exit. There were two elm trees on a hill close enough to each other that we could string a clothesline between them, which we left up during the program. There was a flat space between the trees that became our stage, and the audience could sit on the grass close to the children performing in this space. The director of the summer program brought a large piece of canvas with hooks on it to hang on the clothesline; because it reached the ground, the children could sit behind it and hear everything on the "stage" but not be seen. We worked on not being heard. Behind the flat, the hill dropped off slightly. The children could go behind the flat and sit on the ground while they waited for their scenes.

For each rehearsal, I took the flat down and put it up. I stored it and the costumes and props in the fire department across the road; in fact the firemen became my stagehands, putting it up and taking it down for me, and watched our rehearsals. I kept any thing else I needed in my car.

I also did plays in the backyards of the homes of participating children after the summer program was over. For each site, we adapted this approach. One yard had a badminton net, and I threw two cotton batik bedspreads from India over it for a flat. One yard was in front of a house, with clumps of bushes around. We used those as flats, by draping the same bedspreads over them for entrances and exits.

The best part of doing the plays outside is that the audience sits on the ground. The audience was lower than the children, making the children literally taller and front and center in the experience. Our play notices said to bring a blanket or something to sit on. No chairs were allowed except for anyone who would have trouble sitting on the ground. We placed these on the side so no one's view was blocked. I also learned to bring the audience within inches of where the children would perform. I kept an extra rope with me, which I just laid on the ground as a marker. When we rehearsed, the children knew not to go past it, and the audience knew where to sit. Everyone could see and hear, and sharing the space created a warm and friendly atmosphere in the audience. I never heard anyone say they couldn't hear the children.

### *Rain or a Hurricane?*

While I always worried about rain, the children would bring raincoats and umbrellas for rehearsals and rarely missed a moment. Only once did I experience rain during an outdoor performance in many summers of performing Shakespeare in Wisconsin and Louisiana. It was a slight summer drizzle in Wisconsin. (California does not count, because it never rains in southern California.) The audience had come prepared with plastic bags to sit on and raincoats with hoods. Umbrellas could only be used in the back of the audience. We didn't want anyone to be poked in the eye or anyone's view to be obstructed.

The play was *Macbeth*. Little Lady Macbeth had been stung by a bee on her finger right before we began. A doctor in the house looked at it and put some damp baking soda on it. Tina's eyes were a little teary, and she held the hand with the bee stung finger up with the other one, but when I asked her and the cast if they thought we should go on, she flashed, "I've waited my whole life to play this part and I'm not going to let rain or a bee sting stop me!" (She was nine.) No one else in the cast said a word, and the play went on to rave reviews. The children were damp but happy. Audience members said the rain added to the moody atmosphere of the play, and no one seemed to notice Tina's bee sting, although one member of the audience said, "That little Lady Macbeth was wonderful. It looked like she had tears in her eyes several times and her cheeks were pink with emotion." Or a bee sting. In any case, Tina was grand and so happy her life wasn't over before she got to play Lady Macbeth.

Rain preceding an outdoor performance can be a problem also, as the ground becomes wet. This happened one summer when I was performing *Hamlet* with a group of fifth/sixth-grade students in Baton Rouge, Louisiana. It was August, and hurricane season was approaching. It had rained a great deal for days. We were always able to rehearse because it didn't rain in the morning when we had class, but the ground became very wet and soggy. The children were handling it well, and we discussed what to do about puddles. My main concern, however, was not just that it might pour the night of the performance, but that the ground would be too wet for the audience to sit on it.

Graduate students from LSU were again observing my program as part of an education class they were taking on gifted and talented education. One of them had been in my preservice language arts and reading classes at LSU and was a great help. She threw herself into helping with costumes, running errands, and so on. As the ground grew soggier the day before the performance arrived, she said, "I can fix this. I'll be back in a few hours."

A few hours later Marion was back, driving a pickup truck filled with bales of hay. She was wearing overalls, a cowboy hat, and boots. I had never seen her in anything but a dress. She jumped out of the truck and started throwing bales of hay on the ground. When the casing was off the bales, the hay could be spread over the wet ground like a carpet. I was dumbfounded. She said she had read that they did this during Shakespeare's time when his company of players performed outdoors. It was in one of the books in my Shakespeare library for the children. She had grown up on a horse ranch in the country outside Baton Rouge, and she went home to get the truck and the hay. The night of the performance I acknowledged her, and the children gave her the biggest cheer of the night and lots of hugs. Marion knew the play must go on.

# REHEARSALS

Rehearsals may begin as soon as the play is cast, during the first session. The hardest part at first is not learning the lines, but knowing when to move on and off stage, where to stand, and where to move, as well as using gestures to move, so the blocking of the scenes is really the first thing you rehearse. Sometimes I would just stop and go through the whole play scene by scene, marking these things. The students would enter, place themselves, and exit each scene without even talking to get a good idea of the "road map" of the play.

# Teacher "play notes"

During rehearsals I use a clipboard with a piece of paper and the date on it. As I watch, I make simple "play notes" about things we need to talk about. These may be about anything, from entrances and exits, to costumes and props, to expression and gestures. You may note things that need fixing or things that deserve praise. Praise is good. You may also make notes reminding yourself of something you need to get, a script revision you should make, or whatever you think of as you move toward the final performance.

After each scene, or series of scenes, or a full play rehearsal, we come together as a group and debrief. As you rehearse, the longer you can go without stopping the better, so the children begin to feel what it is like to go through the entire play as they would for a performance. Sometimes you need to stop, but it is always better to let them keep going as long as possible. When you do stop, gather the children together to talk, or debrief, about the rehearsal.

# Debriefing and the only question: "What did you see that you liked?"

Although I have my play notes to share, I always begin with the students. The first thing I do is ask them the only question I ever ask at the beginning of a debriefing session: "What did you see that you liked?" I like to start with the children's comments and save mine for later. Children are used to the teacher praising them. This question also means that your students cannot start criticizing or complaining about other students. The focus should be on what they liked and what worked. It will still allow anyone to make a suggestion about how to make it better, but precludes anyone blaming or making fun of another student.

Sometimes this is a little difficult. During one rehearsal of *Romeo and Juliet*, just about everything that could go wrong backstage in one scene did go wrong. Cues were missed, two children got into an argument and one started to cry, and the prop table fell over. It was very quiet when we debriefed, and I asked, "What did you see that you liked?" There was a very long silence. Finally, one child said, "I like the way Danielle came out on cue."

Ordinarily this would not have been noteworthy, but because almost everything went wrong in this scene except Danielle coming out on cue, it fit. There was a collective sigh, we talked about ways to make it better, and we tried it again.

# Student play books

I asked my students to keep a play book. This could be a small notebook or just pieces of paper stapled together. During each debriefing, they dated the page and took notes on anything they wanted to remember, or jotted down reminders of things I asked them to do or bring to rehearsals.

I notified the parents that they had play books and told students to share them with their parents in case they needed to help the children with something, for example, "my tights ripped—I need a new pair."

# Revising a script as you rehearse

It's all right to revise the condensed script as you begin to rehearse if you see a need. After all, you have already edited the play once, and you can do it again. Depending on your students, you may do any or all of the following.

## *Cut Lines*

If you see that a child handles some lines well and struggles with others, cut the lines that are giving him or her problems, as long as the meaning is not completely lost. Sometimes there are too many lines. At other times, they may not make much sense in a scene, and you can cut them to make the scene flow. You may notice a problem when a child seems glued to one spot, just saying lines. To keep the action flowing, you may need to streamline the scene. The lines should make sense in the scene and be meaningful to the child speaking them and to the other characters in the scene.

If you do cut lines, check to see if this affects another character's lines and adjust the scripts of all the characters affected as well. I found the students would usually do this themselves.

## *Add Lines*

You may also find that a character needs to say more to make the scene flow and make sense to the children. It may sound like something is missing, so add something back. On several occasions I have also had students who had looked at the original play come to me and say, "You cut some of my character's lines." I explained that I had had to cut some things to make the play shorter. If they persisted, I would suggest they revise the scene and add lines, as long as they also adjusted the other characters' lines if necessary.

This happened when I was doing *Julius Caesar* with a group of sixth- to eighth-grade students one summer in Madison, Wisconsin. Beth wanted to be the Soothsayer and thought it would be a very cool part, which indeed it is. She immediately started practicing mysterious movements to depict a strange and exotic character that can tell the future.

However, the Soothsayer didn't have a lot of lines and only appeared in the first scene, telling Caesar to "Beware the Ides of March," and later briefly in the scene where Caesar enters the Senate. She did appear later in the Roman mob, but she wasn't quite satisfied. She showed up the second day of rehearsals and wanted to add the scene where she talks at length to Portia, Brutus's wife, and has a lot to say. I told her that was fine, as long as she cleared it with Portia to see if she wanted to be in another scene. There was also a character named Lucius, a boy, in that scene, who would have to be added. I told her she needed to find someone to play Lucius, because I had not used his character in their script, and coordinate with Portia and Lucius to make the script changes for everybody in the scene.

The Soothsayer, Portia, and Lucius showed up for the third rehearsal, with the entire scene intact as Shakespeare had written it. This started a bit of a snowball effect. Now Calpurnia, Caesar's wife, wanted as many lines as Portia had and began to revise her scenes. Most of the characters were fine with what I had condensed for them, but several started reading the original and revising the script to expand their parts. I knew this would make the play a little longer, but I was excited by their enthusiasm and the fact that they were reading the original play, comparing it to the script I had condensed for them, revising not only the lines their characters said, but those of all other characters in the scene. It was a wonderful mutiny.

In the end, the play ran closer to an hour than the 45 minutes I think should be the maximum for this age group, and it was a little unbalanced—the Soothsayer took as much time with her lines as Mark Anthony did giving his funeral oration over Caesar's body. But in the end this experience should be about the students rather than the audience, the teacher, or even Shakespeare. After the play I told the audience about the students who had contributed to the script revision, also acknowledging their contribution to the whole production in the program. When students are performing in a play by Shakespeare condensed for children, reading the original play, comparing the two, and revising the parts of the characters they are playing and other characters as well, everyone wins.

## *Modify Lines*

You may also modify lines for students. You read about the two brothers in *Macbeth* in chapter 4. The older brother volunteered to be Macduff, but had a language disability and difficulty saying his lines in certain scenes. His little brother played a soldier at his side and said the lines for him. Make such adjustments as you need to, keeping the focus on the students in any play.

## Dress rehearsals

It takes a while to build up to a full dress rehearsal, when everybody has every costume part, all props, and stage weapons and fights if they are in the play. I always tried to have at least three full dress rehearsals before a performance, including the day of the performance, so that students were comfortable in their costumes, efficient at making any costume changes, and knew where to put their props and get them—they often made a prop chart and map themselves, showing where everything was and what scene each thing was used in. This would be posted outside the room or behind the flat so there was no confusion about where anybody's sword, poison bottle, or fan was. It also meant things would not be moved by someone else.

If you are in the classroom and rehearsing on a block schedule, for example, Monday, Wednesday, and Friday, with a performance Friday afternoon and/or evening, this last week would be full dress rehearsal week. This is an exciting time for the children, when they know what they are doing, they are in full costume, and they know the performance is coming up.

# SCHEDULING

Over the years I have found it takes about 18 hours to produce a play. Rehearsals for elementary students in the classroom should be 1½ hours long and may increase to 2 hours when you begin to add costumes, props, and fight scenes. These take more time to prepare, and you need time to get in costume, run the fight scenes or other scenes that take time such as those with dancing, and debrief afterward. For a summer program, I scheduled three plays in three-week sessions: two classes of fourth- to sixth-grade students that met Monday, Wednesday, and Friday from 8:30 to 10:00 and 10:30 to 12:00, and one class of sixth- to eighth-grade students that met Tuesdays and Thursdays from 9:00 to 12:00. We performed all three plays on the last night of the session, at 5:00, 6:00, and 7:00, starting with the youngest group of students at 5:00.

I have found 18 hours to be about the right amount of time to prepare and successfully perform the play. Any less, and they may not be stage ready. There is also a risk in doing more, as they can lose momentum and even over-rehearse, losing some of their enthusiasm and energy.

## Finding time to rehearse

It's natural to ask, "How do you find time to do Shakespeare in an already busy day?" One answer is that language arts and a great deal of content as well can be embedded in this experience. For example, in language arts and reading, you may read aloud from one of the many collections of stories of Shakespeare's plays or the complete play, and students may also read these independently. Students also do independent reading and research for the production of the play and on Shakespeare topics of interest to them. They may write about Shakespeare and the experience of the play they are performing in a journal and discuss Shakespeare books in literature circles. All types of poetry become more interesting to them, and you may read Shakespeare's poetry and other poetry as well or model poetry writing through mini-lessons. Students may write similes, metaphors, and rhyming verse—couplets and quatrains—and learn about and write sonnets. In mathematics you may teach or review place value and relate it to historical periods associated with Shakespeare and the Renaissance by creating time lines. Social studies and science lessons may focus on biographies of Renaissance figures such as Henry VIII, Queen Elizabeth I, or Galileo, and students may research and write about them. They may also research a historical period or the setting of one of Shakespeare's plays and write a historical newspaper, for example a fictionalized newspaper from ancient Rome if they are performing *Julius Caesar*. Students learn arts content as they do inquiry-based projects related to the play to add music and dance, to increase understanding of theater stage craft and the visual arts as they make set designs and props, design programs, or illustrate reports they write. They also learn to use technology by doing online research on Shakespeare and the play they are performing, participating in online discussion boards, or doing Shakespeare WebQuests.

In my own classroom I found that we maximized the use of time and it was used to advantage, as much at the urging of my students as my own. They were so engaged in performing Shakespeare, so focused and intense, that the metabolism of the entire school day was raised.

I found that doing Shakespeare could boot my class to warp speed. Everything moved faster when I sighed heavily, shook my head slowly, wore a world-weary expression on my face, and said, "If only we could just finish [whatever needed to be done] more quickly, we'd have more time for Shakespeare." Then the fur would fly, the fur being checking homework or finishing a math assignment, wrapping up peer-editing conferences, or simply clearing tables before lining up to go to recess. Because they were so enthusiastic and engaged, I found they would focus on a task and also help each other. Students often came to school early, begged to stay in class to rehearse at recess and lunch, or were reluctant to leave in the afternoon. On occasion, I told them they needed to get a life.

Here are some of the practical ways in which teachers can make time for performing Shakespeare:

- ❖ **Home:** Students learn lines outside of school time. I have had students and parents practice in the car or with other students on the phone. They would keep scripts handy and run lines whenever they had a chance.

- ❖ **Groups:** Students form scene groups to rehearse during a language arts block, rotating with other reading or writing activities. I often found them doing this during their free time, recess, lunch, and before and after school.

- ❖ **Block scheduling:** Once rehearsal of the whole play is underway, I use a block schedule two to three times a week, rather than every day. This gives them time to think about and process what happened during a rehearsal, learn any needed lines, add gestures, or work at home or in groups. On nonrehearsal days, other subjects are taught during the block.

- ❖ **Rehearse and perform in the classroom:** If you block and rehearse a play in the classroom and perform it there in the round as well, you do not waste valuable time traveling to a stage; moving costumes, sets, or props; or waiting if the stage is being used.

- ❖ **Team teaching:** Another teacher and I traded classes, and we both taught to our strengths. I did Shakespeare with her class; she taught mine math. We found it to be a remarkable time management strategy. We set a tight schedule with high expectations. Her students complied readily because they were happy to be doing Shakespeare. My students complied readily because they were happy I was not teaching them math.

## Scheduling whole-class rehearsals

It is best to rehearse at least an hour at a time at the beginning and rehearse every other day to give students time to work on lines before the next rehearsal. As you move closer to the performance, a 1½- or 2-hour rehearsal will give you time to move through the whole play from beginning to end, with time for talking and making adjustments. You can still rehearse every other day, leaving time for students to work on individual scenes between whole group rehearsals or prepare costumes and props. You may also want to rehearse every day right before the performance.

In the classroom, I used a block schedule (see figure 5.1). On the days we didn't rehearse, we used the block for social studies or science. I also scheduled rehearsals in the afternoons because I found that Shakespeare energized students, who sometimes drag as the school day wears on. We did reading, writing, and mathematics in the mornings, and then alternated Shakespeare rehearsals with social studies and science in the afternoons.

| Monday | Tuesday | Wednesday | Thursday | Friday |
|---|---|---|---|---|
| Language Arts/Reading | Language Arts/Reading | Language Arts/Reading | Language Arts/Reading | Language Arts/Reading |
| Recess | Recess | Recess | Recess | Recess |
| Mathematics | Mathematics | Mathematics | Mathematics | Mathematics |
| Lunch | Lunch | Lunch | Lunch | Lunch |
| Block: Shakespeare, 1 or 1½ to 2 hours | Block: Content Area, Social Studies, Science, etc. | Block: Shakespeare, 1 or 1½ to 2 hours | Block: Content Area, Social Studies, Science, etc. | Block: Shakespeare, 1 or 1½ to 2 hours |

**Figure 5.1. Sample block classroom schedule**

# Small group scene rehearsals

Often students can rehearse a particular scene in a small group. I have found they like to do this and will often volunteer, and we find a time for them. You can't always spend all the time you or they would like on one scene, because you want to keep the rehearsals moving toward rehearsing the play all the way through. Also, if you stop and work through one scene, other students are not as engaged.

This may be done during reading or writing workshop or any other group work time. I have found children will do this on their own at recess, lunch, or after school, or at home if they can get together. They have even told me they rehearsed over the phone.

One "problem" I had as a teacher was that students came to the classroom early to rehearse or wanted to stay after school, if they didn't ride a bus, to rehearse, leaving me with less time to prepare or unable to leave the classroom. I decided that this was a good problem to have, within reason.

A Final Word

Children come early and stay late to rehearse Shakespeare. Or as one child put it during a summer program, "I liked everything about doing Shakespeare except when we took breaks."

# CHAPTER 6

# Producing a Play

This chapter provides ideas for costumes, sets, and props, based on two guiding principles:

❖ Keep it simple.

❖ Let the children do it.

Stories and examples of students reading and researching production elements show how to keep performances student-centered, and that the things needed for play production should not distract attention from the children.

## KEEP IT SIMPLE

One of the many wonderful things about Shakespeare's plays and performing them with children is that the play production can be very simple. Shakespeare gave very few stage directions. The Globe Theatre was a thrust stage that extended somewhat out into the audience, which stood very close, the "groundlings," with one exit and one entrance and a trap door, which was sometimes used for ghosts to appear. There was a balcony at the rear of the stage for musicians.

His plays don't need a lot of costuming, props, or backdrops, because his language is so descriptive. We "see" things because he tells us what they look like. It's not uncommon for modern theaters to stage Shakespeare with no sets or props and with actors simply dressed in black.

When I started doing Shakespeare with children, I saw how this would allow me to focus on my students and Shakespeare's words rather than objects, and I liked that. I also liked that the simplicity of dressing a set or an actor while doing Shakespeare meant that my students could do this themselves, with guidance from me and resources I could provide (e.g., books and images of historical clothes and costumes), as well as images of play productions and the way magic and fantasy was depicted. (See appendix A.)

My students became engaged—dare I say "obsessed"—with reading about Renaissance or Greek and Roman clothing or medieval weapons, sketching ideas for their own costumes, and writing descriptions and lists of what they would need to find, on their own or with a parent's or my help. Dress is a form of self-expression, in real life and in drama.

**Figure 6.1. Vintage sketch of stage of Shakespeare's Globe Theatre**

Students really spent more time dreaming, reading, and talking about costumes and theater props than creating or using them. Items found at home are more than enough to outfit a play. A child's imagination is the best source of sets and costumes, for it can handily transform some cardboard room dividers into Macbeth's impenetrable castle and a few broken branches with children crouched behind them into the entire English and Scottish armies. A pair of black tights topped with a mother's belted tunic blouse changes anyone into a Renaissance rake. A child in a light-colored leotard decorated with puffs of colored nylon net attached to the back straps with twist ties for wings is obviously a midsummer fairy.

The most important thing is to keep the costuming simple and the focus on the students. You can suggest general ideas to them, but also let them research and make decisions about their specific costumes.

I remember working on lighting/sets/costumes and having the play come alive through the process of creating that scenic climate as much as working on the lines of the play. I never felt we privileged the text over the scenic elements; in fact, I think we had a sense of and appreciated the role of scenic elements in supporting the story.

Felicia Roberts, in Carole Cox's fourth/fifth grade class,
Shorewood Elementary School, Madison, Wisconsin, 1968–1969

# COSTUMES

In this section are some general ideas for costumes I have used to help students create Renaissance and medieval, classical Greek and Roman, and magical costuming, with specific ideas for each of the ten plays suggested for children in chapter 2.

Some of the plays strongly suggest a type of costuming. We almost always picture *Romeo and Juliet, Twelfth Night,* or *The Taming of the Shrew* in a flamboyant, colorful red, blue, and gold Renaissance style. *Hamlet,* however, is often done in dark Renaissance colors or black modern dress, and could also take a more medieval look, as could *Richard III. Macbeth* could be medieval, even primitive, and definitely Scottish, with muted tartan fabric. *Julius Caesar* is usually done in classical Greek and Roman style, but I have seen many productions that use a modern military style suggestive of a government dictatorship.

Some plays seem more open to a choice in styles, such as *A Midsummer Night's Dream.* Because it is set in ancient Athens, I have always done it with children in the simpler classical Greek and Roman style, plus magical for the fairy kingdom, because it is the easiest to do with children. But we also see it done in the style of Shakespeare's time, with Renaissance costumes on the Athenian royalty, young lovers, and workmen. If a play is set in Greece or on an island, I prefer the simpler classical Greek and Roman costumes. These plays would be *A Midsummer Night's Dream, The Comedy of Errors,* and *The Tempest.* With Shakespeare, it really is up to the director, and that would be you.

## Renaissance and medieval costumes

*Romeo and Juliet*

*Hamlet*

*The Taming of the Shrew*

*Twelfth Night*

*Richard the III*

*The Comedy of Errors*

*A Midsummer Night's Dream*

*The Tempest*

**The casts of *Romeo and Juliet* and *Hamlet* in Renaissance costumes**

## *Colors*

For flamboyant Renaissance style, use deep jewel colors like red, blue, emerald, turquoise, fuchsia, and gold. Hamlet himself is usually dressed in black, but the rest of the cast may be in bright colors. Burgundy and navy also work well for royalty or older characters in Renaissance-setting plays. I use lots of ribbons in these colors as well, which may be attached to a costume very simply in several ways and give it a Renaissance flair.

## *Male Renaissance Costumes*

### Basic costume of blouse, belt, tights, and shoes

Picture the silhouette of padded shoulders and full sleeves, a narrow waist, padded hips, and narrow legs, with the addition of a cloak, hat, or sword. Children, boys or girls playing boys, may begin with an adult woman's blouse with full, long sleeves and any kind of collar, including a peasant blouse, and reaching about the top of the leg on a child. Use any kind of belt at the waist. Worn over colored or black tights, the longer blouse will cover their hips. Add any kind of sandal (not a flip flop) or ballet or jazz shoes, and that is all you need. You may vary the colors of the blouse and tights to suggest rank—purple for royalty or black for age—or in the case of *Romeo and Juliet*, family affiliation (e.g. red for the Capulets, Juliet's family, and blue for the Montagues, Romeo's family). This is a basic costume, but you may build it up by adding other things:

## Vests

Begin with a simple vest to add more interest or another color. A short piece of twisted fabric wrapped with different-colored ribbons and attached around each armhole with a few stitches builds up the shoulders and gives a finished look. Attach ribbons to hang freely to just below the elbow for a dashing detail.

## Armbands and garters

Make an armband from elastic to fit just above the elbow: measure, cut, and secure it with one stitch. Cover it with ribbon and tie a bow on the outside, letting various colored ribbons hang from the bow like streamers. Make a garter the same way, to fit just above the knee on one leg only.

## Pouches

Use a small cloth bag, like the kind department store makeup giveaways come in, or make one with a drawstring and attach it to the belt. Add ribbon streamers.

## Shorts

If the blouse does not cover the hips, or for older students, take a pair of gym type or running shorts and make a casing for elastic around each leg, run elastic through it, secure the elastic to the right length to make the short leg look puffy, and have them wear it over tights. I have found that girls especially want to wear shorts over their tights when playing a male character. Black shorts are usually fine, or a contrasting color to the tights.

## Hats

Young characters may go hatless or wear a beret. Older characters like fathers or dukes may wear a beret with a piece of fabric wrapped around it like a turban, with a piece of fabric hanging from it to the shoulder on one side; continue the fabric under the chin to the other side if that works. You can use different types of fabric on each hat. It's not necessary to sew it, except a few stitches to secure it to the hat. Add feathers or flashy costume jewelry brooches, pins, or a dangly earring to suggest wealth. Thrift shops often have vintage women's pillbox hats that will work for a male character, and you may add to them as described for the beret.

One caution about hats: don't let them get in the way. I once had a fifth-grade boy playing Mercutio in *Romeo and Juliet* who had spent his own money buying a vintage pillbox woman's hat that was a deep blue velvet. He was very proud of it. It looked great as a costume piece, but it kept falling off. We all watched tensely during every rehearsal to see if the hat would fall off. I told him that if it did, he should just leave it on the ground, but that obviously distracted him. We finally settled on a plan. He wore the hat when he entered the scene, took it off when he bowed to another character, and casually tossed it aside into the bushes to continue the scene. My advice is, if a hat keeps falling off, leave it off.

## Drapes and cloaks

A piece of fabric a few feet long may be bunched on one shoulder, draped diagonally across the chest, and secured through the belt on the other side. Use appropriate colors: a purple drape would suggest royalty; a black one would indicate age or wisdom. Cloaks are fine, but they sometimes overwhelm a smaller student and even get in the way of movements. If they are homemade, they also sometimes look like a costume at Halloween—Dracula or Superman. The best cloak I ever had I bought at a St. Vincent DePaul thrift store in Madison, Wisconsin. It was from a nun's habit and had a high collar that closed easily and fitted shoulders with slits for arms rather than sleeves, and was full enough, with gores, to swish wonderfully. It was short enough so that it didn't drag. I used that cloak in every play.

## *Female Renaissance Costumes*

### Basic costume of high-waisted, long dress

Picture the silhouette of a high, empire-style waist, long, almost straight skirt, and either long or short puffy sleeves. Sometimes these are called "granny dresses," and I have found women's nightgowns that are not sheer that have this silhouette. I have also used bridesmaid's dresses I found at garage sales or thrift shops. If a dress is too long, cut it and stitch it, use double-face tape, or just leave it unhemmed. Don't cut it with pinking shears, however.

### Accessories for the dress

Use samples from an upholstery store; they come in pieces of about a foot square. Ask for old sample books. These are often in brocade patterns in rich colors and even metallic threads. Choose one that looks good with the dress and simply tack it with a stitch at each corner of the neckline where it meets the sleeve. This adds interest, texture, and a richer look. If the sleeves are short and puffy, put a leotard or other long-sleeved top underneath and add ribbons in an armband right under the puffy part with ribbon streamers, as described for male Renaissance costumes above.

### Shoes

Ballet shoes, jazz shoes, flats, and sandals all work.

### Hats

A pillbox shape is ideal. Find these at thrift shops, or use the forms for bridal headpieces found at fabric stores. Attach a scarf or length of nylon net in the back just above each ear, letting it dip down in the middle, and let the ends also hang down, for a great Renaissance look hat. You can do this with a beret or any other hat with a round, head-hugging shape and no brim. Add feathers or costume jewelry if the character is wealthy.

### Jewelry

Use costume jewelry chains in multiples or chains with medallions, or center a brooch on the neckline of the dress.

## *Male Medieval Costumes*

**Medieval costumes, swords, and shields: Macbeth and Macduff in *Macbeth***

Picture a more primitive look than the Renaissance, with an unfitted tunic top with a belt at the waist over leggings, sweatpants, or longer shorts. This look is for *Macbeth* but could also be used for *Hamlet* or *Richard III*.

### Tunics

Use a piece of upholstery or other heavy fabric the width of a child from elbow to elbow with arms held out to the side, and length from knee to knee. You don't need to finish or sew the edges, just cut them (but not with pinking shears). Fold this in half width-wise, find the center of the fold, and make a very small cut a few inches on each side, or just big enough to pull over the child's head. Don't make the cut too big, or it will flop around and slide over the shoulder. Cut a little bit at a time, and you may make a vertical cut in the middle front as well. This will make a simple tunic that can be belted over a long-sleeved T-shirt or sweatshirt. It's fine if the sweatshirt has a hood; that may be part of the costume, either on the outside of the tunic or on the head with a strip of leather around the forehead. Use muted neutral colors: brown, beige, gray, or olive. Worn fabric looks good, as if the character has spent nights sleeping in the heather, on the moor, and so forth.

### Leggings

Sweatpants or workout clothes or yoga pants cover the legs. Avoid bright colors or deep black. If the colors are too bright, wash the leggings with bleach to take some of the color out. You can also put dance leggings that just come to the knee over sweatpants.

### Drapes or cloaks

See the suggestions for Renaissance male costumes, but choose heavier, more muted, rougher-looking fabric and dark cloaks. I've even had students throw an old worn blanket over one shoulder if the fabric and color blended well with the costume.

### Shoes

Fairly heavy sweat socks in gray or beige may be worn with a bulky sandal, or use short boots.

### Armbands or wristbands

Use a width of fairly heavy fabric to wrap around the upper arm if a sleeveless T-shirt is used (in the summer, for example) and secure it with leather strips. Or make a wristband the same way. These can be tricky to keep on, so if they fall off, leave them off.

### Headbands

A leather strip or a strip of heavy fabric straight across the forehead looks great.

## *Female Medieval Costumes*

The silhouette is a long-sleeved, long dress and can be a looser fit than the empire-waist Renaissance dress.

### Dress or robe

With a lighter fabric than the tunic for the male characters, such as muslin or a dark cotton or polyester, use the same method to cut it, only it should be full length. This may be belted using a belt or a longer length of ropelike or braided fabric trim that will go around the waist twice and then hang down in the front to at least the knees. The robe may be worn over a dark leotard and dark tights or light leggings, so it does not require side seams, but it needs sleeves, and everything must be covered. I have found great women's robes at thrift shops that have a loose-fitting shape; we added the long belt that hangs in front.

### Shoes

Ballet or jazz shoes, flats, and boots work well.

### Headband

A piece of the same braided trim may be worn as a headband. A piece of dark net or a scarf may be attached in back.

### Accessories

Use heavy costume jewelry such as a bracelet cuff, heavy chains, or medallions.

# Classical Greek and Roman costumes

*Julius Caesar*

*The Comedy of Errors*

*A Midsummer Night's Dream*

*The Tempest*

## *Colors*

White is the basic color, but other colors may be added, depending on the character. For example, Julius Caesar may have an additional length of purple fabric over the right shoulder, or even just a length of purple fabric over his right arm bent at the elbow. Other deep, dark colors may be used to distinguish one character from another, such as dark blue, dark green, or burgundy.

## *For Male and Some Female Characters*

Draped white cloth in the classical Greek and Roman style of a toga, or a garment called a *chiton*, is the basic costume for these plays. A child may wear an adult-sized white T-shirt that comes to about the knees. To make a drape over it, use a length of lightweight fabric that drapes well. Fold it in half lengthwise. Where it folds, it goes on one hip, with a length of cloth in front and back of the shoulder opposite the hip. It should be loose fitting. Tie the two ends of the drape at the shoulder with white ribbon or fabric trim, and let one end hang down in front and the other in the back. Sandals complete this basic classical look.

**Helena wears a *chiton* in *A Midsummer Night's Dream***

## A *Chiton*

A *chiton* was more like a tunic and was a very traditional style of dress in the ancient world. It may also be worn over a large white T-shirt. It may be made several ways, from sheets or any lightweight fabric. (See figure 6.2a through d.) Use two lengths of fabric, from the shoulder to at least the knees and about as wide as elbow to elbow on a child with arms outstretched. Attach the fabric at the shoulder. There will be excess on each side, which will hang down. It doesn't need further sewing or attaching anywhere, but a belt may be added.

If you want to have fabric that drapes over the top like a collar, add length, drape it over front and back to about mid-chest, and then attach. This piece can also be trimmed with a color at the edge.

For a female character, you could also use a soft pastel color and make it floor length with a leotard and skirt or shorts underneath. For an older character, use a dark color such as brown, grey, or burgundy.

Let children research a *chiton* and decide how to make their own.

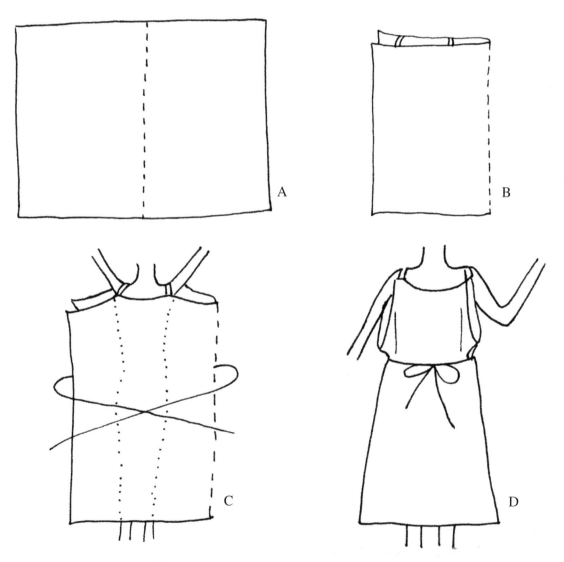

**Figure 6.2a through d. Making a *chiton***

### Headwear

A crown of laurel leaves may be made from a length of plastic leaves for any or all classical costumes. For *The Comedy of Errors*, which takes place in the seaside town of Ephesus in Greece (not necessarily ancient Greece as in Julius Caesar), students may tie a strip of cloth across their foreheads or even wear berets. The same is true of *A Midsummer Night's Dream* and *The Tempest*. For these two plays, you may add magical costumes for the supernatural characters.

### Shoes

Use sandals, not thongs.

## *For Female Characters*

Female characters like Calpurnia, Caesar's wife, may wear a full-length *chiton* in white, or, because she is Caesar's wife, purple. A colored drape could be added. Calpurnia could also go all out and wear gold lame. Other female characters who could wear this costume are Miranda in *The Tempest*, the women in *The Comedy of Errors*; and Queen Hippolyta, Titania, and the young women in *A Midsummer Night's Dream.*

### Headwear

A gold, braided fabric trim may be used as a circlet across the forehead or on the head as a crown. Silver and other colors may be used to differentiate characters.

### Jewelry

Look for costume jewelry that will add to a classical look: wide cuff bracelets, collar-type necklaces, chandelier earrings, and rings with a large stone.

# Magical costumes

*A Midsummer Night's Dream*

*The Tempest*

*Macbeth*

The first two plays have a less-defined time and place, and you may do anything with the witches in *Macbeth*. You may use costumes in the period styles described above and add magical elements, or create something new all together.

## *All Magical*

I like to begin with the simpler classical costumes with both the first two plays, adding magical elements for the magical characters. In *A Midsummer Night's Dream*, the Athenians may wear classical or Renaissance costumes, and in *The Tempest* all the characters may begin with these basic costumes. I've used both classical and Renaissance costumes for most characters in *The Tempest*. You could even do a combination of styles by using Renaissance for the characters who are shipwrecked on Prospero's island, but classical for Prospero and Miranda, who live on the island. Prospero is also a wizard, so you could add a tall hat or a turban or something to signify that he has magical powers. He may also wear a loose robe or a cape.

**Titania, the Fairy Queen, and fairies wearing *chitons* in *A Midsummer Night's Dream***

## *Specific Magical*

Following are ideas for specific magical characters in these plays.

### *A Midsummer Night's Dream*

❖ **Fairies.** My simplest fairy costume starts with a tank bathing suit or leotard in a solid, lighter color. Add a poncho of nylon net. Cut a piece of net as wide as elbow to elbow when a child holds his or her arms out to the sides and as long as knee to knee (see previous description). Fairies may also wear *chitons*. Take a length of net, fold it in half lengthwise, then take a long twist tie, put it under the strap, and twist it around the length of net about 5 inches down, to make a little pouf for the top part of the wing. Add ballet slippers or sandals.

The King and Queen of the Fairies may wear classical dress, and you may add bigger net wings. Crowns may be made from plastic leaves in a circlet and worn across the forehead or further back on the head.

❖ **Bottom.** Bottom is one of the workmen in the enchanted forest at night, practicing a play for the wedding of the Duke. Puck magically gives him an "ass's head" and then makes Titania, the queen of the fairies, fall in love with him, because Oberon, the king of the fairies, is mad at her. Find or make a donkey or horse mask and twist plastic flowers around the ears. One of the teachers who used to observe me as a part of graduate classes at LSU made one I used for years. She shaped a head with chicken wire, including ears, leaving holes for eyes. She covered the whole thing with gray velour stretchy fabric and added long, black felt eyelashes. Extra fabric covered the child who wore it about down to the collar bone.

**Bottom with an ass's head in *A Midsummer Night's Dream***

## *The Tempest*

❖ **Ariel.** This character is a magical spirit and may wear a fairy costume as described above, or whatever a child can imagine. It's a magical sprite.

❖ **Caliban.** This character is a kind of monster, and there is a description of the way the monster looks, but I think anything goes here. He may wear a tunic with attached rags or fake fur. He should look like he lives outdoors in the forest, unkempt and dirty.

## *Macbeth*

❖ **Witches.** These are generally not pointy-hat witches, but rather hags that live in a cave on the moors in Scotland. A poncho with dark "rags" hanging off it, or just a dark poncho, will work. Children may wear a leotard or tank suit underneath. One year my summer group performed *Macbeth* in a Shakespeare Family Festival that was held in the early evening before each performance of the Shakespeare Festival/LA. It was outdoors in the Japanese garden of the VA hospital in Westwood, near UCLA. The witches were wearing leotards and ponchos of cheesecloth dyed grey, with raggedy strips hanging off them. There was a pond near where we performed, and the witches got into patting mud on their arms and legs and ratting their hair and putting leaves and twigs into it. They looked like they had just crawled out from under a rock. They looked great.

**Macbeth watches the witches dance, in *Macbeth***

# Modern: any play

You don't have to do a certain historical period, with literal costumes, such as Renaissance for *Romeo and Juliet*, or make sure fairies have wings. I have always done these more traditional types of costuming because I thought my students liked it, and I do, too. But Shakespeare's plays have been costumed in many different ways.

## *Other Historical Period*

I saw an amateur adult production of *A Midsummer Night's Dream* with my students, in a park in Long Beach with 1960's-style costumes. Puck was dressed as a "beatnik," in all black and a beret. Oberon and Titania were dressed as John and Jackie Kennedy. My students didn't care for it, and I think the historical references eluded them. On the other hand, Baz Luhrman's film of *Romeo and Juliet* was set in a contemporary city near the sea in a warm climate. Friar Laurence wore a Hawaiian shirt. The students I was doing Shakespeare with at the time loved it.

## *Nontraditional Ideas*

These are costume styles I have seen in adult productions that could be done with children.

### All Black

Contemporary or any historical style, all black: T-shirts or turtlenecks, shirts, pants, blouses, dresses, tights, or leggings. *Hamlet* is sometimes done this way. It could also work for *Macbeth*, with the addition of tartan drapes, as well as *Richard III*. He is almost always shown in black, so the whole cast could follow suit. Costume pieces to signify a character, such as a large neck chain for Hamlet or Richard, or hats or capes for some characters, could provide interest. It certainly would be simple to tell everyone to come dressed in black.

### Thematic or Symbolic

I have seen *Julius Caesar* at the Old Vic in London done in a contemporary quasi-military style reminiscent of uniforms in Hitler's Germany or Mussolini's Italy during World War II—brown shirts and pants, arm bands with a nationalist symbol (not necessarily a swastika), boots, and military hats or caps. It could also be done in khaki or camouflage. I saw a production of *A Midsummer Night's Dream* at the renovated Globe Theatre in London done as a slumber party—the female characters wore baby doll pajamas and nightgowns, and the male characters were in flannel pajamas. I think the idea was that it was all a dream.

# SETS

See chapter 5 for ideas about staging a play in a classroom or outdoors. The only thing that is needed, besides moving the desks in the classroom, is a "flat" that children can stand behind and that creates one exit and one entrance, in addition to a classroom door.

This flat can be, but does not have to be, decorated as a scene. The easiest thing is to keep it a solid color. You may drape fabric over it as an accent, depending on the play. For example, use a light blue or green drape with vines and leaves attached for *The Tempest*. There is only one thing I have used as set decoration, and only in certain plays: a wooden picnic bench with no back or arms. I use it in *Romeo and Juliet* so the Nurse can sit down, Romeo can stand on it during the balcony scene, and Juliet can die on it in the last scene, covered by a large piece of cheesecloth or net as a shroud. It could also be used for Julius Caesar's body, covered with a shroud—a large piece of cloth. I've learned it's too much to expect a child to stay dead throughout this whole scene. It's best to cover them. It could be used in other plays as well if you want to create interest by having some characters sit down, or put one leg on it while they are standing up and talking, for example in *Hamlet*, *The Taming of the Shrew*, *Macbeth*, *Richard III*, or *Twelfth Night*.

The bench is unobtrusive, but if you have a small space and it gets in the way, don't use it. *The Tempest* has such a feeling of being out in nature on the island that I don't think you need a bench. There is so much running around in *A Midsummer Night's Dream* or *The Comedy of Errors* that you want the space empty with no obstacles. *Macbeth* has a big battle scene at the end, so if you need the space, don't use a bench. Again, keep it simple. Don't use set decoration if it doesn't make sense. Shakespeare didn't.

# PROPS

Use as few props as possible. They often get in the way and distract from the children and Shakespeare's words. The only essential props are weapons if you plan to do certain plays. *Macbeth*, *Romeo and Juliet*, and *Hamlet* have important fight scenes. Richard III needs to wave a sword in the last battle, but the actual fight could take place offstage. There are many ways to find appropriate stage weapons for plays.

## Stage weapons

There are two things I learned not to do about stage weapons. The first was not to use cardboard swords. They simply don't work because they are not sturdy enough. The second is not to use wood or wooden dowels, which seemed to be working well until one broke in half and we were all staring at a really sharp, long, and dangerous splinter.

I have, however, had lengths of aluminum dowels cut and added a cross piece at one end, strapped on with leather strips. They are easy to make, they don't break, they are silver, and they clang nicely.

There are several ways to find appropriate stage weapons. Try contacting the drama department at a college or university or a community theater group. I have also used weapons that a fencing teacher and coach loaned me. There are heavy, plastic toy weapons that look realistic.

## Fight Scenes That Require Weapons

Certain plays really require weapons for a fight, not just as part of a costume.

### Hamlet

Hamlet needs a sword to kill Polonius behind a curtain, which is not really a fight. Hamlet and Laertes have a fight at the end, and just about everyone dies. The style of weapon would be a Renaissance foil used in fencing.

**Laertes and Hamlet prepare to fight, as Claudius and Gertrude watch, in *Hamlet* (eighth graders)**

**Sword fighting, in *Hamlet*: Laertes and Hamlet (nine- to eleven-year-olds)**

### *Romeo and Juliet*

Tybalt and Mercutio fight, then Tybalt and Romeo fight, and Renaissance-type foils would be used. Juliet needs a small dagger to kill herself.

**Romeo and Tybalt fight with swords, in *Romeo and Juliet***

### *Macbeth*

The English army sneaks up on Macbeth's castle, hiding behind branches and then fights, with the Scottish army. They can use a more medieval-style weapon, shorter and with a broader blade. Many toy swords look like this. Macbeth and Macduff have a fight at the very end, and their swords should be heavy enough to look realistic and make some noise.

Doing Shakespeare in your summer programs has had a lasting impression on me and I have a very vivid memory of being handed the kick-ass shield and sword that I would use as Macbeth.

Scott Ryder, in Carole Cox's "Shakespeare for Kids" summer program in
Baton Rouge, Louisiana, 1980, 1981, 1982, and 1983

My mother's "Shakespeare for Kids" program was something that I did not completely understand at first. Much of the language was difficult for me and the responsibility, as a participant, a bit more than I was capable of handling at the time. The whole thing seemed like some elaborate operation that was preventing me from doing nothing at all during the summer.

Then I was told that swords would be involved. It was then I started to shut up and pay attention. I strapped on those turquoise tights and rolled through the dirt, swinging my trusty piece of aluminum, doing my best to poke a classmate, and later, I hacked away with proper broadswords and a trusty shield. I dove over, under, and through bushes with my magic rapier, ready to slay any nemesis with a fatal underarm strike. I was particularly excited to make my entrance, as a chain-mail-wearing MacDuff, by scaling a wall and then dropping down in the arena. The thrill of battle then, pumped me so that I made the fake throat slice a little too real and perhaps broke the skin of my tiny enemy, Macbeth.

It was then that I started to realize that a summer without Shakespeare was one that I did not want. The final performances have faded from my memory, but the few weeks of rehearsals were the most fun anyway. Cutting up backstage (behind bushes), not completely following directions, and enjoying time with my friends through much of the summer really helped me not only, perfect my robotic, monotone flair for the dialogue, but also helped me be a happy kid. I had a chance to hold one of those now very tiny rapiers in my mother's garage not long ago, and in my hand, it felt like a great summer. It was then that I started to realize my mother just wanted a bunch of kids to have some fun. Thanks, Mom.

Wyatt Cox, in Carole Cox's "Shakespeare for Kids" summer program,
Baton Rouge, Louisiana, 1980, 1981, 1982, and 1983

# LIGHTS, MUSIC, AND SPECIAL EFFECTS

In general, keep it simple. It is very easy for lighting, music, and special effects to distract from the children. Avoid anything that is likely to go wrong or is just too difficult for children to do themselves. There are some simple things, and a few more complicated, that I've used successfully over the years.

## Lights

If you do a play indoors in the classroom or a multipurpose room or gym, simply turn lights on and off for effect. You would probably be doing the play during the day or early evening, so the room would not go completely dark.

For example, I did this in my classroom for *Macbeth*. The lights were turned off when Lady Macbeth came in to do her mad scene. Martha had asked me if she could carry a candle as she was sleepwalking. I thought it was a good idea but was a little worried about her trying to handle the candle and deliver her lines. Instead, we decided the Doctor and Gentlewoman would come in during the scene, holding candles. They had fewer lines , and the effect was the same. We also flicked the lights off and on during the witches' scene when Shakespeare's stage directions say, *Thunder. Lightning.* We rattled a piece of aluminum for the lightning. You could also go dark and use a candle when Hamlet encounters the Ghost of his father.

I've used flashlights with red cellophane over the bulb to simulate torches in *Julius Caesar.* Members of the mob listening to Mark Anthony carried them, and when he roused them to anger, we dimmed the lights and they lit their "torches."

If you do a play outdoors, you will do it before it gets dark. However, I've used little white Christmas lights when I had access to electricity and a long enough cord, to give the set a magical look. They look great just strung randomly in trees and bushes.

# Music

Music can be part of any play by Shakespeare performed by children. See appendix A for sources of recordings, information about using music, and songs.

I always tried to have music produced by the children in the plays. A simple tune played on a recorder by a child in a scene or backstage can be wonderfully effective. Ask students if they play any instruments and try to integrate them into the play. I hit the jackpot one summer when we were doing *A Midsummer Night's Dream.* I had children who were learning to play recorder, flute, violin, and French horn. Gordon played the French horn when King Theseus arrives, when it says *Horns*, and he also played during the farcical play done by the workmen. Because it was a comedy, the fact that he was just learning to play and it was supposed to be funny worked. Elizabeth was Puck, and she played the violin in the wedding scene. I also used bells on leather straps for the workmen's dance at the end.

Find out what the children are able to do, then build on their interests and talents. There are so many songs in Shakespeare's plays that may be simply spoken, but if a child or a group of children can sing, as Laura did in *Macbeth* as Hecate, goddess of the night, be sure to use their talents. I did *Twelfth Night* once in Madison, and one of the children in the group was part of a boy's choir that his mother directed. She brought the choir to sing during the pre-performance Renaissance Festival, and her son sang during the play. She also worked with other children on songs.

# Special effects

The only special effect I have ever used is dry ice in the witches' pot in *Macbeth,* besides using ketchup for the blood on Lady Macbeth's hands (it works great). I was nervous about using the dry ice but got advice on how to do it, and it meant a great deal to the first little witches I tried it with, so I continued to do it. You need to use a heavy pot with a handle so the witches can start the ice bubbling backstage and carry the pot onto the stage. I have used a heavy Dutch oven, the kind you can find in camping stores. The ice should be stored in a metal container in the pot. Children should not touch it with bare hands, and they should use oven mitts to handle the container. The top of the container may then be removed while it is still in the pot. To create a bubble effect, a child may slowly pour room temperature water over the ice and carry the pot onstage. I have also had the pot partly hidden by a bush, with the water in an old-looking container and poured on during the scene. It will bubble for a few minutes, sending out what looks like a heavy ground fog like you see in horror movies. Don't do this if you are hesitant, but I found that my witches became incredibly independent and powerful when they had the responsibility of making magic ice turn into fog.

## A Final Word

Nothing should divert attention from the children. If a hat keeps falling off, leave it off.

# CHAPTER 7

---

# Performing a Play

This chapter describes how to keep the focus on children by being well-rehearsed, playing in a safe venue, giving children responsibility, avoiding distractions, and dealing with an audience. Ideas for programs and publicity, as well as researching, planning, and staging a Renaissance Fair before a performance, are included, along with examples of student-produced programs and publicity.

## KEEP THE FOCUS ON CHILDREN

The most important thing about performances is that the focus is on children. This also means they take responsibility for a performance. I quickly learned that as long as my students looked to me for cues for when to move in and out of a scene, or told them forgotten lines, or reminded them about costume changes or behavior in front of the audience and especially offstage, they would not learn to do it themselves. I gradually released responsibility to them for the success of the performance and explicitly told them what their responsibilities were—not just for what they would do in the play, but how they would work together and cooperate with each other to be successful.

### Be well-rehearsed

I would never put children in front of an audience unless they were well rehearsed enough to do everything themselves. It takes about 18 hours of preparation to be ready to perform the play. See chapter 5 for suggestions on rehearsals and a schedule. I found they could be performance ready in this amount of time.

By the last week of rehearsals, they should be able to go through the whole play without stopping, even if everything isn't perfect. It's hard to be perfect. That would be about three complete dress rehearsals. If there are scenes that need some work, polish these scenes at another time. Students in these scenes may work in small groups.

The last week should also include full costume dress rehearsals with all props and special effects, just the way you plan to do the final performance.

## Preview performances

I always planned a preview performance, with an open invitation to parents and other family members to come. These were really still rehearsals, but children step up their game when there is an audience, even one person. These were usually not crowded because they were held during the day, either during the school year with my own elementary class, or at the regular class time during a summer program, and parents might be working, or busy, or choose to wait for the final performance. I also had family members attend who might have had a conflict with the time of the final performance, or the elderly, ill, or handicapped, because it was easier to make special accommodations with a small audience. Parents have also attended these previews with small children instead of bringing them to the final performance, where they might prove to be a distraction. I have also had the "press" at these previews so they could freely move about and take photographs, which I would not allow during the final performance.

These previews put everybody on their best behavior. I also used a video camera myself to kick up the performance level a notch. Sometimes I didn't even turn it on, but they didn't know that. It was clear they wanted to do their best in front of the camera. In addition, I told them that because I was filming, I would not stop them or give them any help. They really could do this on their own, and they always did.

Dear Elizabeth, Gordon, and cast members,

I wanted to let you know how much I enjoyed your preview performance of *A Midsummer Night's Dream*. I know you noticed how much I was laughing. I understood what was going on because you delivered your lines with clarity and feeling and the interaction between the characters was very lively.

Elizabeth, I liked both the parts you played. It was fun to watch you as a fancy-free fairy. However, your interpretation of the lion was memorable. One moment, he was being ferocious and the next minute he was making me laugh out loud with his "lion dance" to the beat of a conga line.

Gordon, your performance as Puck was great. I enjoyed your soliloquies and the little bits of mischief you did. You really showed the humorous side of love.

Alice (The laugher), in a letter written to cast of *A Midsummer Night's Dream*, at Carole Cox's "Shakespeare for Kids" summer program, Long Beach, California, 1991

## Choose a safe venue

As I described in chapter 5, we always performed the play where we rehearsed it so that everything was familiar and safe for the children. I tried moving a performance once; things did not go very well, and I never did that again. Safe venues would be your own classroom, or a space such as a library or multipurpose room where you can consistently schedule time and not have any distractions.

**Figure 7.1. A sign made by a student to direct the audience to the play**

In a school, be mindful of the time bells will ring, potential announcements over the intercom, or fire or other emergency drills. If your students are waiting to enter a scene in the hall, ask other teachers to reroute classes that might pass by.

When I taught summer classes, I tried to find a place away from street noise or people walking by, although this is not always completely possible. I did find, however, that people were sensitive to what we were doing, especially if I told them they could watch if they sat down and were quiet.

When I did the summer program on the playground of my school in Madison, the firemen across the street, who helped me by storing my flat and costumes, frequently wandered over to watch, but stood close to the sidewalk as though they were guarding us. The sight of a first responder in uniform standing watch must have had a settling effect on people walking by.

One summer I did *Macbeth* on the campus of Louisiana State University when I was a professor there. There is a space behind the student union with a tall, slightly curved wall which is a monument to Huey P. Long, governor of Louisiana in the 1930s. There is also a large, round concrete platform with curved concrete benches on each side, and I thought it was a perfect setting for *Macbeth*. It had the look and feel of a castle, walls and all. My students sensed this as well and surprised me when Wyatt, the boy playing Macduff, who was supposed to come out from behind the wall and challenge Macbeth to fight during the last scene, actually appeared on top of the wall, yelling "Tyrant show they face!" at Macbeth, who couldn't locate him at first. Then Wyatt, a very athletic Macduff, dropped from the wall. Other students behind the wall had hoisted him up. I was horrified at first, but they assured me they could do it and it was safe. We left it in as a great bit of theater. But this space was on a corner with street traffic, and college students wandering by. I worried about this, but needlessly. The students in the play learned to really project their voices over the traffic sounds. They actually enjoyed the college students watching, and we had regular attendees. I asked them to sit on the ground and be quiet if they watched. They monitored other students walking by. Some of our groupies came every day.

## Give children responsibility

I learned to trust children doing Shakespeare and to give them responsibility. I never go backstage, and I never prompt after a few rehearsals after we "drop scripts." I tell them that if they forget a line, they must think on their feet and improvise. I caution other children in the scene to give that person time to reflect and make the save, but to use their good judgment if they can assist with the save. I tell them that they are much more familiar with the play than anyone in the audience, even adults, and the audience won't know the difference.

I can remember many times when this happened. The audience doesn't notice if the cast can make a good recovery. Students other than the one who forgot the line learn to flip the forgotten line into a question. They have also said part of their lines and paraphrased when they forgot the exact wording.

The most notable example of how the audience doesn't notice is when we were doing *The Taming of the Shrew* in Madison. This was a group of fourth- to sixth-grade students, and there was some flirting going on between the girl playing the shrew's younger sister Bianca, whom everyone wanted to marry, and the boy playing Lucentio, the one she really liked in the play. In fact, they were so busy flirting backstage on the night of the performance, they missed an entire scene in which the other suitors see her talking with Lucentio. The suitors said their lines and waited in vain. They moved around a little bit to create some business to stall, but after a minute or so, one made the save and said something like, "I think Bianca and Lucentio are up to something, and we need to find out what it is." He then left the stage, at which point Bianca and Lucentio finally remembered to enter, but seeing the stage empty, they walked across the stage holding hands as though nothing had happened. I knew they were upset and embarrassed afterward, but I told them it was fine, they had all done a great job covering up, and no one noticed! I was watching the audience, and they didn't notice. We talked to numerous people, who said they didn't notice any missing scene.

One of my cardinal rules is no adults backstage. I remember as a child when a volunteer parent barred me from going on stage because she didn't understand a cue, even though it was my turn to go on. My teacher had to walk across the stage and rescue me. Too many times I watched my own children, who frequently participated in school music and drama programs, being misguided by volunteer adults, or I saw adults making themselves so visible that it looked as though the students couldn't do the show themselves. They can and should be allowed to do so.

I tell them at the beginning of rehearsals that I will not be there to help them during the performance. I say I plan to stand at the back of the audience where they probably can't even see me, so they need to be responsible for everything themselves. I do this for two reasons. First, I found I got so nervous while they were performing that I was afraid I might communicate this to them, or let my nerves get in the way of good judgment if something happened. Second, I also found that if they couldn't see me, they wouldn't look for me or depend on me, and would just do it themselves. And they always did.

When we have debriefing discussions after rehearsals, we discuss everything that is happening both on and off stage. We decide together where people exit and enter, so that Macbeth leaving the stage doesn't bump into Banquo entering after Macbeth has sent the murderers to kill Banquo. We usually establish a kind of circular flow so that characters enter one way and exit another. We also need to determine if they need to enter from a certain place for the next scene they are in. All of this is carefully planned, and they know what to do.

I am also never backstage, so they cannot rely on me for their cues. We see where there might be problems and make plans accordingly, which they carry out. It can be confusing and noisy at first, but we work on that. And I never, ever have anyone—parent, friend, sibling—backstage who is not in the play.

Children learn to monitor their own behavior if we support them and give them the opportunity. I have seen them create, entirely on their own, a poster with pages of the script in order and stage notes showing where to enter and exit and who and what props are needed. They have also drawn maps for each scene, with arrows and notes to remind themselves. Students responsible for lights or helping others with props create their own lighting and prop scripts. All of this is really important to advocate for drama and Shakespeare in your classroom. Students are engaged, learn to take responsibility, and are held accountable. In fact I think this is one of the reasons they love doing Shakespeare so much. They, not the teacher or parent or anyone else, are doing it. They own it. It's theirs.

# No distractions

Try to eliminate as many distractions during a performance as possible. When performing a play in the round in your classroom, your adult audiences can be seated in student desks or on chairs in a circle around the perimeter of the room. Audiences of students in other classes may be seated in a circle on the floor. For outdoor performances, the audience may be seated on the ground. In this way you have the advantage of the audience being close enough to hear well—and not shouting "we can't hear"—and they are below the standing students in the play. The students can look over their heads, not at their faces. I think they feel more important that way, and won't be as likely to break character as they would be if family members were mouthing words at them or getting tears in their eyes. I advise them to look over the heads of the audience, not at any one person, and they see the sense in that. Because the audience is either on the perimeter of the room with no one in front of them, or on the ground looking up at the students, there are no chairs scraping or being moved around, or people stretching and moving around to see.

I encourage parents with babies or really small children to bring them to a preview performance near the end of rehearsals, not the final performance. Similarly, if they have a relative or friend in a wheelchair or walker or who needs assistance, a preview might be best. I always arrange to have reserved seat chairs for anyone who needs assistance and place them on the side or back of the audience.

I make it clear to everyone that no one will be seated after a performance begins, and they should not leave during a performance. The students know who is coming, so we can wait to start if we know someone is on the way.

Finally, no cameras. I sometimes face resistance to this, but I explain that they wouldn't go see a Broadway show or any other live theater performance and stand up and take a flash photo; this shouldn't be any different. They can take pictures at previews, and if they can't come to those, I will take pictures or set their video camera up for them at a final rehearsal. No cameras.

## PROGRAMS AND PUBLICITY

Students will create publicity without you even telling them. They will bring drawings for the cover of a program. They can design and prepare the program themselves. You may give them information you would like included, but they may do this themselves by hand or using a word processor. They may also create posters, notices to newspapers for the event section, or notices for the school newsletter or announcements over the PA. An e-vite could be sent out via the Internet.

I have also contacted newspapers to see if they would like to do an article, and without exception they have. This has happened in Madison, Wisconsin, Baton Rouge, Louisiana, and Long Beach and Los Angeles, California. In Madison we were written up as a review of live theater in the arts section. In Baton Rouge, when we were rehearsing on the LSU campus, the local television crew

**Figure 7.2a and b. Examples of student-created program covers**

showed up and told us they had heard about us, asking if they could film us. I got permission from parents, and they did a really nice piece on the local news, with videos of our rehearsals, interviews with me and the children and parents, and the final performance. In Long Beach, local papers always wrote about us, and so did a university newsletter. A radio producer heard about us and did a show, which aired around the country on National Public Radio. When we were the opening act for the Shakespeare Festival/LA, we were in the *Los Angeles Times*.

All of this is wonderful for the students, who work very hard to do these plays, whether they are writing and producing the programs and publicity themselves, or others are writing about them.

# A PRE-PERFORMANCE RENAISSANCE FAIR

As I saw my students read, research, and learn about the Renaissance and Shakespeare's theater, I thought of doing a pre-performance Renaissance Fair, because they were very interested in learning about the world at that time. I thought it would be a minor event, but the students were often as engaged with this fair as if it were the performance itself. I also opened it up to participation by other family members so that they were engaged in the project as well. We had many volunteers and some wonderful events. See appendix A for many ideas for creating a Renaissance Fair.

## Ideas for audience participation in a Renaissance fair

We first sent out invitations to our Renaissance Fair, with ideas for family and audience participation. Students did research and worked hard on this, making specific suggestions, most of which were followed at one time or another. The only thing we never had was a dancing bear, although someone came in a high school mascot bear costume with a Renaissance cap one time, danced around, and was a smash. Following are some of the things you might suggest.

### *Come in Renaissance dress*

Anyone can come in Renaissance dress, even if it 's a hat or a cape or flowers in the hair. I have been amazed at how many people will really get into the spirit of the fair and dress in Renaissance style. The invitations could include sketches of Renaissance clothing that children could research and draw for ideas.

### *Music*

I always have taped Renaissance music ready. But I have also invited people to be "strolling musicians" and play any musical instrument. People have participated with guitars, flutes, ukuleles, drums, trumpets, and saxophones. On one occasion a child in the play brought her violin to play, and the sister of another cast member also brought hers. Since they were about the same age and playing level, they had learned some of the same pieces and could play them together.

### *Food and Drink*

Food is easy, so anyone can participate. I suggest that the children or family members bring treats such as cookies, brownies, fruit, cupcakes, etc. They put them in a basket or on a tray and decorate it with ribbons or flowers, to pass around.

**A young guest and a fairy in *A Midsummer Night's Dream* play violins during a pre-performance Renaissance Fair**

In their research, my students found the types of foods that were popular at theater events in Shakespeare's time and made suggestions for these on the invitation as well. One of these was gingerbread, and we have used the following recipe for gingersnaps, which was given to me by one of my students at Shorewood Hills Elementary School who was in the first class I did Shakespeare with. It was her grandmother's recipe from Germany. We also learned to make copies of the recipe to hand out because many people asked for it:

## Gingersnaps

- ¾ cup shortening
- 1 cup sugar (brown or white), plus ½ cup white sugar for rolling dough balls in
- 1 egg
- 4 tbsp molasses
- 2 cups flour
- 2 tsp baking soda
- 1 tsp each ground ginger, cloves, and cinnamon

Preheat the oven to 350°F.

Cream the shortening and sugar. Add the egg and molasses and combine.

Sift the flour with the baking soda and add to the wet ingredients, then add the ginger, cloves, and cinnamon. Mix until a soft dough is formed. Chill until firm, about 1 hour.

Roll the dough into balls and then in sugar. Arrange them evenly on a greased cookie sheet. Bake at 350°F for 10 to 12 minutes.

During one of the summers I did "Shakespeare for Kids" outdoors in Baton Rouge, education graduate students observed and also participated in the program as a required field experience for a course taught by another professor at Louisiana State University. They came to observe and participate and write a short report of the experience.

I asked them what they would do to participate specifically, after some seemed to think it was a time to drink coffee and chat while sitting on the grass watching me work with students. I gave them some ideas, and they decided they would help the students plan and coordinate the Renaissance Fair. It became a real extravaganza with their support. They helped every child participate in some way.

Since I had a lending library of books for the program in plastic crates, they used these books to work with the children. One of the things they found out was that mead, a fermented drink made from honey, was popular in Shakespeare's time. So they made a huge batch of mead and served it with a dipper before the play. It was a hit, and everyone wanted refills, but we had to shut down the mead stand when someone realized that it really had fermented, explaining the full-bodied taste and aroma, which were due to the alcohol content. Needless to say, it was a memorable Renaissance Fair.

## *Flowers and favors*

Children found out that at real Renaissance Fairs, things like flowers and craft items were sold. We didn't sell things, but many times students brought baskets of flowers picked from their gardens or made garlands of vines like ivy to wear in the hair, and passed these out. Several times children made potpourri and put it in small squares of net tied in ribbons, offering these sachets in baskets at the Fair. One child wrote quotes from Shakespeare on small pieces of paper torn to look like parchment and offered these. Another child made wreaths of ribbons and other ribbon ornaments to wear in the hair.

## *Performance arts*

My students also discovered that there were performers at Renaissance Fairs: jugglers, acrobats, magicians, storytellers, and animals. They suggested these as well on the invitation, and some of my students became pre-performance artists, doing magic tricks, juggling, songs, and handstands. We have also had yo-yos and jump rope tricks, mimes, a pet gerbil in one of those big plastic balls, and dancing – from ballet moves to break dancing. Some made a sandwich board poster to wear listing Shakespeare's sonnets. A theater patron could pick a sonnet, and the child would read it; sometimes the child had memorized it.

The Renaissance Fairs became a highlight of the performances. I originally planned for 30 minutes before the play, but we extended that to an hour before the play, and it was rare if it didn't pick up again after the performance. It was a wonderful opportunity not only for the students to extend the experience of performing in a play, but for family, friends, and members of the community to also participate.

# COMMUNITY SUPPORT

Ask for community support for the performance and the Renaissance Fair and acknowledge it in the program:

❖ Newspapers and television: Announcements, reviews, and articles

❖ Stage weapons: university or college drama departments and local theater groups.

❖ Fabric stores: donations of fabric and trims.

❖ Flower shops: fresh single stem flowers to pass out at the Renaissance Fair

❖ Lumber yards, hardware stores, and building supply stores: materials for weapons and other props

❖ Office supply stores: paper and photocopying

❖ Used bookstores: paperback editions of the plays

❖ Librarians are the best, and will scour the shelves for books related to Shakespeare, the Renaissance, costuming, and stagecraft.

# A Final Word

**Question:** How did you feel about playing King Duncan and a soldier in *Macbeth*? (Carole)

**Answer:** Happy, happy, happy, happy, happy, . . . and proud. (Ryan, eight years old)

# Appendix A: Resources for Children and Teachers

This is a selectively annotated list of resources for teaching Shakespeare through performance, for grades 3–8. It includes books for children and young adults that a teacher could use to build a classroom Shakespeare library. Although many of the titles are current, older versions of stories of his plays are often republished by various publishers, and new books on Shakespeare are published all the time. He is a topic that never seems to grow old. For example, there are numerous recently published graphic versions of his plays, including those in the Japanese manga style. As for some of the older books, which might be out of print, they can still be found on public and school library shelves or through interlibrary loan. Web-based sources for used books, such as Amazon (www.amazon.com), Powell's bookstore in Portland, Oregon (www.powells.com), and ABE Books (abebooks.com) could also be a source of out-of-print books.

There are books and ideas for teaching Shakespeare and Web sites that provide background information on Shakespeare that might be of interest,. None provides a complete guide to performing a play, which is one of the reasons this book has been written. You may find useful information, resources, ideas for playing scenes, and related teaching ideas in them that could complement performing a play.

It is most important to build a classroom library on Shakespeare when students are performing a play. They will read widely from the books in a classroom library and engage deeply in specific research to help with the play production. They will learn about Shakespeare's plays, his language, and his world as they live through the experience of performing the play.

Encourage your school media center librarian to develop a real concentration in this area and then offer it to classrooms to supplement what they have, as a rotating collection.

## BOOKS FOR CHILDREN AND YOUNG ADULTS

These books could be included in a classroom library for student independent reading or researching some aspect of performing the play. The list could also be given to a school or public librarian to help you build a classroom Shakespeare library. On page 98 is a memo for parents with suggestions for extending the classroom experience of performing one of Shakespeare's plays, as well as a selected list of books and Web sites from the complete list in this section.

# Shakespeare and Your Student

**Extend the Experience of Performing Shakespeare**

- Talk to your students about the play and their parts.

- Read lines and play scenes with them.

- Read books about Shakespeare and his plays.

- Explore Shakespeare on the Internet.

**Stories of the Plays**

Chute, M. *Stories from Shakespeare.* New York: Meridian, 1993.

Claybourne, A. *Usborne Stories from Shakespeare.* Tulsa, OK: EDC Publishing, 2005.

Lamb, C., and M. Lamb. *Tales from Shakespeare.* New York: Random House, 2007.

Matthews, A. *The Random House Book of Shakespeare Stories.* New York: Random House, 2001.

Nesbit, E. *The Best of Shakespeare.* New York: Oxford University Press, 1997.

Packer, T. *Tales from Shakespeare.* New York: Scholastic, 2004.

Williams, M. *Bravo, Mr. William Shakespeare!* Cambridge, MA: Candlewick Press, 2000.

Williams, M. *Tales from Shakespeare.* Cambridge, MA: Candlewick Press, 2004.

**Shakespeare and His World**

Aliki. *William Shakespeare and the Globe.* New York: HarperCollins, 1999.

Chrisp, P. *Shakespeare: An Eyewitness Book.* New York: DK Publishing, 2004.

Claybourne, A., and R. Treays. *World of Shakespeare.* London: Usborne, 2004.

Mannis, C. D. *The Queen's Progress: An Elizabethan Alphabet.* New York: Viking, 2003.

Rosen, M. *Shakespeare: His Work and His World.* Cambridge, MA: Candlewick Press, 2001.

Ross, S. *Shakespeare and Macbeth: The Story Behind the Play.* New York: Viking, 1994.

Stanley, D., and P. Vennema. *Bard of Avon: The Story of William Shakespeare.* New York: Morrow, 1992.

Stanley, D., and P. Vennema. *Good Queen Bess: The Story of Elizabeth of England.* New York: Morrow, 2002.

**Shakespeare-Inspired Fiction**

*Grades 3–5:*

Francis, P. *Sam Stars at Shakespeare's Globe.* London: Francis Lincoln, 2006.

Rogers, G. *The Boy, the Bear, the Baron, the Bard.* New Milford, CT: Roaring Brook Press, 2004.

*Grades 6–8:*

Blackwood, G. L. The Shakespeare Stealer Series. New York: Dutton, 2004. (upper elementary and middle school)

Broach, E. *Shakespeare's Secret.* New York: Henry Holt, 2005.

**Web Sites**

www.absoluteshakespeare.com. Summaries and complete texts of the plays, and more

www.folger.edu. The Folger Shakespeare Library in Washington, D.C.

www.shakespeare.palomar.edu. Annotated links to Shakespeare on the Internet

From *Shakespeare Kids: Performing his Plays, Speaking his Words* by Carole Cox. Santa Barbara, CA: Libraries Unlimited. Copyright © 2010. May be copied for classroom use.

## Stories of the plays in collections

There are many collections of stories of Shakespeare's plays, and these stories have been around since Charles Lamb and Mary Lamb first published *Tales from Shakespeare* in 1807. This book continues to be published by various companies in both hardback and paperback versions. Similarly, the stories from Shakespeare written by Edith Nesbit, a well-known English children's author who died in 1924, continue to be published. For these and other authors of these stories, I have tried to include recent or most recent editions. Each collection contains different plays, and some are highly illustrated. These may be read aloud to students or read independently.

Birch, B. *Shakespeare Stories: Comedies.* New York: Peter Bedwick Books, 1988.

———. *Shakespeare Stories: Histories.* New York: Peter Bedwick Books, 1988.

———. *Shakespeare Stories: Tragedies.* New York: Peter Bedwick Books, 1988.

Chute, M. *Stories from Shakespeare.* New York: Meridian, 1993.

Claybourne, A. *Usborne Stories from Shakespeare.* Tulsa, OK: EDC Publishing, 2005.

Garfield, L. *Shakespeare Stories.* New York: Houghton Mifflin, 1991.

———. *Shakespeare Stories II.* New York: Houghton Mifflin, 1995.

Lamb, C., and M. Lamb. *Tales from Shakespeare.* New York: Random House, 2007.

Matthews, A. *The Random House Book of Shakespeare Stories.* New York: Random House, 2001.

McCaughrean, G. *Stories from Shakespeare.* New York: Margaret K. McElderry/Simon & Schuster, 1995.

Miles, B. *Favorite Tales from Shakespeare.* New York: Macmillan, 1985.

Nesbit, E. *The Best of Shakespeare.* New York: Oxford University Press, 1997.

———. *Green Tiger's Illustrated Stories from Shakespeare.* Seattle, WA: Green Tiger Press, 2009.

Packer, T. *Tales from Shakespeare.* New York: Scholastic, 2004.

Serralier, I. *Stories from Shakespeare: The Enchanted Island.* New York: Henry Z. Walck, 1964.

## Stories of a single play

These illustrated stories of a single play are in picture book format. These books may also be read aloud to students or read independently.

Beneduce, A. K. *The Tempest.* New York: Philomel, 1996.

Coville, B. *William Shakespeare's* Hamlet. New York: Dial, 2004.

———. *William Shakespeare's* Macbeth. New York: Dial, 1997.

———. *William Shakespeare's* A Midsummer Night's Dream. New York: Dial, 1996.

————. *William Shakespeare's* Romeo and Juliet. New York: Dial, 1999.

————. *William Shakespeare's* The Tempest. New York: Delacorte, 1994.

————. *William Shakespeare's* Twelfth Night. New York: Dial, 2003.

Early, M. *The Most Excellent and Lamentable Tragedy of Romeo and Juliet.* New York: Harry N. Abrams, 1998.

Hopkins, A. *Romeo and Juliet.* New York: Barnes & Nobles Books, 1998.

Lamb, C., and M. Lamb. *A Midsummer Night's Dream.* New York: Franklin Watts, 1972.

Matthews, A. *Hamlet: A Shakespeare Story.* London: Orchard Books, 2003.

————. *Macbeth: A Shakespeare Story.* London: Orchard Books, 2003.

————. *A Midsummer Night's Dream: A Shakespeare Story.* London: Orchard Books, 2003.

————. *Richard III: A Shakespeare Story.* London: Orchard Books, 2003.

————. *Romeo and Juliet: A Shakespeare Story.* London: Orchard Books, 2003.

————. *The Tempest: A Shakespeare Story.* London: Orchard Books, 2003.

————. *Twelfth Night: A Shakespeare story.* London: Orchard Books, 2003.

Mayer, M. *The Tempest.* San Francisco: Chronicle Books, 2005.

Rosen, M., and J. Ray. *Shakespeare's Romeo and Juliet.* New York: Candlewick, 2004.

## <u>Shakespeare Explained</u> series

Each of the books in this series includes a literary analysis and summary of the play, background information on Shakespeare, and the history and culture of Elizabethan England; the series is more appropriate for upper elementary and middle school students.

Anderson, R. *Macbeth.* Tarrytown, NY: Marshall Cavendish Children's Books, 2009.

Naden, C. J. *Romeo and Juliet.* Tarrytown, NY: Marshall Cavendish Children's Books, 2009.

Sobran, J. *Hamlet.* Tarrytown, NY: Marshall Cavendish Children's Books, 2009.

————. *Julius Caesar.* Tarrytown, NY: Marshall Cavendish Children's Books, 2009.

————. *A Midsummer Night's Dream.* Tarrytown, NY: Marshall Cavendish Children's Books, 2009.

## <u>Usborne reading</u> series

The series is intended to be used as part of a reading program, but could be read aloud by teachers or read independently by students as well.

Claybourne, A. *Romeo and Juliet.* Tulsa, OK: EDC Publishing, 2006.

Mason, C. *Macbeth.* Tulsa, OK: EDC Publishing, 2006.

Simes, S. *A Midsummer Night's Dream.* Tulsa, OK: EDC Publishing, 2006.

# Shakespeare's poetry in collections

**Kastan, D. S., and M. Kastan, eds.** *William Shakespeare*: *Poetry for Young People Series*. Falls Church, VA: Sterling, 2000.

> This is an annotated collection of Shakespeare's sonnets and famous soliloquies, each illustrated with realistic color paintings.

**Mayhew, J.** *William Shakespeare, to Sleep, Perchance to Dream: A Child's Book of Rhymes*. New York: Scholastic, 2001.

> Well-known rhymes from Shakespeare's plays and poetry were chosen for young children in this collection.

# Shakespeare and his world

**Aagesen, C., and M. Blumberg** *Shakespeare for Kids: His Life and Times*. Chicago: Chicago Review Press, 1999.

> An introduction to Shakespeare and Elizabethan England, with background and activities, plus how to make things from the period, such as a pomander ball, a juggler's beanbag, and games.

**Aliki.** *William Shakespeare and the Globe*. New York: HarperCollins, 1999.

> The book chronicles the building of a replica of the Globe Theatre in London by Sam Wanamaker and lets the reader see what it must have been like in Shakespeare's time.

**Ashby, R.** *Elizabethan England*. New York: Marshall Cavendish, 1999.

> An introduction to sixteenth-century England and a cultural history of the Golden Age of the Renaissance there through poetry, Shakespeare's theater, art, architecture, and music.

**Bailey, G., and K. Faster.** *Shakespeare's Quill*. New York: Crabtree, 2008.

> An interesting twist on information about Shakespeare's life and times, told in a contemporary story about two children who learn from an antique dealer who loves Shakespeare.

**Beccia, C. 2008** *The Raucous Royals: Test Your Royal Wits: Crack Codes, Solve Mysteries, and Deduce Which Royal Rumors Are True*. Boston: Houghton Mifflin, 2008.

> Among the many historical rumors examined in this humorous, highly illustrated, and entertaining book are several pertaining to Shakespeare: King Richard murdered his nephews; Henry VIII was so fat that he had to be carried by his servants; rumors about Henry's six wives; and Mary Queen of Scots plotted to assassinate her cousin, Queen Elizabeth I.

**Berne, E. C.** *William Shakespeare: Playwright and Poet*. Edina, MN: Abdo Publishing, 2008.

**Brown, J. R.** *Shakespeare and His Theatre*. New York: Lothrop, Lee & Shepard, 1982.

**Cavendish, M.** *Shakespeare's England*. New York: Marshall Cavendish, 1989.

> The life and times of Shakespeare, Henry VIII, and Queen Elizabeth I.

**Chrisp, P.** *Shakespeare: An Eyewitness Book*. New York: DK Publishing, 2004.

> Full of facts about Shakespeare, from the Elizabethan way of life to how the plays were staged. Highly illustrated with photographs and drawings. This book could be useful in planning play production with children.

**Claybourne, A., and R. Treays, R.** *World of Shakespeare*. London: Usborne, 2004.

> A guide to Shakespeare's life, his works, and his influence on the world today. This is an Internet-linked book.

Ferris, J. *Shakespeare's London.* New York: Kingfisher, 2000.
> This is written like a travel guide to the city during Shakespeare's time and includes a detailed foldout map.

Greenhill, W. *Shakespeare's Theatre.* Chicago: Heinemann Library, 2000.
> Describes Shakespeare's theater, staging, and acting.

————. *Shakespeare: A Life.* Chicago: Heinemann Library, 2000.
> Shakespeare's life and times.

Hilliam, D. *William Shakespeare: England's Greatest Playwright and Poet.* New York: Rosen Publishing Group, 2005.
> A biography focusing on Shakespeare's works.

Hodges, C. W. *Shakespeare's Theatre.* New York: Coward McCann, 1964.

Horizon Magazine, eds. *Shakespeare's England.* New York: American Heritage, 1964.

Langley, A. *Shakespeare's Theatre.* Oxford: University of Oxford Press, 1999.
> An illustrated history of the Globe Theatre through its reconstruction in modern times by American actor and director Sam Wanamaker, using paintings by Jane Everett, who was the "artist of record" for the project.

Lace, W. *Elizabethan England.* San Diego: Lucent Books, 1995.

Rosen, M. *Shakespeare: His Work and His World.* Cambridge, MA: Candlewick Press, 2001.
> A description of the world Shakespeare lived and wrote in as well as brief stories and histories of the plays.

Ross, S. *Shakespeare and* Macbeth*: The Story Behind the Play.* New York: Viking, 1994.
> This book tells the fascinating backstory of how Shakespeare came to write *Macbeth*, often called "The Scottish play," after Queen Elizabeth had died without an heir and King James I, the son of Mary Queen of Scots, ruled England. When the king requests a performance at the palace, we see how Shakespeare's plays were produced and how important it was to have a powerful patron like the king.

Ryan, P. *Shakespeare's Storybook: Folktales That Inspired the Bard.* New York: Barefoot Books, 2001.
> The connections between this collection of folk and fairy tales, ballads, and historical events to several of Shakespeare's plays are explained.

Stanley, D., and P. Vennema. *Bard of Avon: The Story of William Shakespeare.* New York: Morrow, 1992.

Turk, R. *The Play's the Thing: A Story about William Shakespeare.* Minneapolis, MN: Carolrhoda, 1998.

"William Shakespeare, Master Playwright." *Calliope* (A Cobblestone Publication) 15, no. 8 (April 2005).
> This 48-page issue of *Calliope* includes articles for children and young adults on Shakespeare's life, theater, how plays were staged, and more. Go to the Folger Shakespeare Library Web site (www.folger.edu/store) to order a copy; you may also order this from the publisher.

# Queen Elizabeth I of England

**Adams, S.** *Elizabeth I: The Outcast Who Became England's Queen.* Washington, DC: National Geographic Society, 2005.

**Crompton, S. W.** *Queen Elizabeth and England's Golden Age.* Philadelphia: Chelsea House, 2006.

**Hilliam, P.** *Elizabeth I: Queen of England's Golden Age.* New York: Rosen Publishing Group, 2005.

**Hinds, K.** *Elizabeth and Her Court.* Tarrytown, New York: Marshall Cavendish, 2008.
> A social history of the royal court of Elizabeth I.

**Kirtland, G. B.** *One day in Elizabethan England.* New York: Harcourt Brace Jovanovich, 1962.

**Mannis, C. D.** *The Queen's Progress: An Elizabethan Alphabet.* New York: Viking, 2003.
> A beautifully illustrated alphabet book with nuggets of information about the age of Elizabeth for younger students, told as an account of Queen Elizabeth I's annual holiday, known as a "royal progress."

**Stanley, D., and P. Vennema.** *Good Queen Bess: The Story of Elizabeth of England.* New York: Morrow, 2002.
> A reissue of a celebrated picture book biography of Queen Elizabeth I, appropriate for younger students.

**Thomas, J. R.** *Behind the Mask: The Life of Queen Elizabeth I.* New York: Clarion Books, 1998.


# Shakespeare-inspired fiction

This is an eclectic list, from humorous and fanciful wordless pictures books and story books for younger students to historical and contemporary young adult fiction, all with one thing in common: Shakespeare. These books are appropriate for grades 5–8, unless otherwise noted.

**Blackwood, G. L.** *Shakespeare Stealer.* New York: Dutton Children's Books, 1998.
> A 14-year-old orphan boy is apprenticed to a man who orders him to infiltrate Shakespeare's acting troupe to steal a script of *Hamlet*, a common practice in a time before copyright laws. Instead, the boy discovers the meaning of friendship and loyalty.

———. *Shakespeare's Scribe.* New York: Dutton. Children's Books, 2000.
> This is a sequel to *Shakespeare Stealer.* In plague-ridden England in 1602, a 15-year-old orphan boy, who has become an apprentice actor, goes on the road with Shakespeare's troupe and finds out more about his parents along the way.

———. *Shakespeare's Spy.* New York: Dutton Children's Books, 2003.
> This is a sequel to *Shakespeare Stealer* and *Shakespeare's Scribe.* The young orphan apprentice actor finds out who has been stealing from Shakespeare's company.

———. *The Shakespeare Stealer Series.* New York: Dutton Children's Books, 2004. All three books in the series are in this one volume.

**Broach, E.** *Shakespeare's Secret.* New York: Henry Holt, 2005.
> The author makes liberal use of the historical details surrounding William Shakespeare's life to explore the possibility that Edward de Vere, Earl of Oxford, may have been the true author of the works attributed to Shakespeare.

**Cheaney, J. B. *The Playmaker*.** Alfred A. Knopf, 2002.
A 14-year-old apprentice in Shakespeare's company helps uncover a plot against Queen Elizabeth I.

**———. *The True Prince*.** New York: Alfred A. Knopf, 2002.
In this sequel to *The Playmaker*, the young apprentice becomes involved in another conspiracy, this time involving Shakespeare's company.

**Cooper, S. *King of Shadows*.** New York: Margaret K. McElderry Books, 1999.
In this time travel story, after a young actor playing Puck in Shakespeare's *A Midsummer Night's Dream* to celebrate the opening of the renovated Globe Theatre in London in modern times becomes ill, he awakens from a fever and finds himself in sixteenth-century London, playing the part of Puck in Shakespeare's company.

**Francis, P. *Sam Stars at Shakespeare's Globe*.** London: Francis Lincoln Children's Books, 2006.
An illustrated story book for younger students about Samuel, who joins Shakespeare's company and plays roles for children: Puck, Cobweb, the grandson of Corilanus, and a young Roman boy in *Julius Caesar*. His dream is to play Juliet. The book is a vivid historical recreation that explores the convention of boys playing girls' parts in sixteenth-century England. Grades 3–5.

**Koertge, R. *Shakespeare Bats Cleanup*.** Cambridge, MA: Candlewick, 2003.
When the 14-year-old main character, whose life revolves around baseball, is homebound with an illness, he begins to read and explores sonnets and other poetic forms to write about his life. He dreams of becoming a baseball star.

**Meyer, C. *Loving Will Shakespeare*.** New York: Harcourt Children's Books, 2006.
Historical fiction based on the courtship and marriage of Shakespeare and Anne Hathaway.

**Rogers, G. *The Boy, the Bear, the Baron, and the Bard*.** New Milford, CT: Roaring Brook Press, 2004.
This humorous, wordless picture book set in the Globe Theatre during Shakespeare's time shows a child on a stage mysteriously transported to Shakespeare's time, where he meets a bear and frees a baron from the Tower of London, all the while being chased through the streets of London by Shakespeare. Grades 3–5.

**———. *Midsummer Knight*.** New Milford, CT: Roaring Brook Press, 2007.
In this companion to *The Boy, the Bear, the Baron, and the Bard*, the bear has an adventure with the same boy, baron, and Shakespeare, in a magic forest not unlike the one in *A Midsummer Night's Dream*. Grades 3–5.

**Vining, E. G. *I Will Adventure*.** New York: Viking, 1962.
A boy's adventures take him to London in 1596, where he meets Shakespeare himself.

# Graphic books

Several publishers have used the contemporary style of graphic books/novels and manga to retell the enduringly contemporary themes of Shakespeare's plays with a new energy, to engage a new generation of readers with accessible and graphically rich versions. These books are more appropriate for students in grades 6 to 8 and are generally found in the young adult section of the library. The two books by Marcia Williams are in a highly illustrated, graphic comic book style, but are appropriate for elementary students in grades 3–5.

# *Grades 6–8*

## <u>Manga Shakespeare</u> series

This is a trendy, edgy, and imaginative take on Shakespeare's plays in the manga style. In the retelling of *Macbeth*, samurai warriors have reclaimed a future, postnuclear world of mutants.

Appignanesi, R. *Manga Shakespeare:* Romeo and Juliet. New York: Amulet, 2007.

———. *Manga Shakespeare: Hamlet.* New York: Amulet, 2007.

———. *Manga Shakespeare: Julius Caesar.* New York: Amulet, 2008.

———. *Manga Shakespeare: Macbeth.* New York: Amulet.

Brown, K. *Manga Shakespeare: A Midsummer Night's Dream.* New York:: Amulet, 2008.

Duffield, P. *Manga Shakespeare: The Tempest.* New York: Amulet, 2008.

## <u>No Fear Shakespeare</u> series

This graphic novel series uses a blend of illustrations and text for each play.

Babra, N. *Hamlet.* New York: Spark Publishing, 2008.

Hoshine, K. *Macbeth.* New York: Spark Publishing, 2008.

Spark Note Editors. *Julius Caesar.* New York: Spark Publishing, 2003.

———. *A Midsummer Night's Dream.* New York: Spark Publishing, 2003.

———. *The Taming of the Shrew.* New York: Spark Publishing, 2003.

———. *The Tempest.* New York: Spark Publishing, 2003.

———. *Twelfth Night.* New York: Spark Publishing, 2003.

Wiegel, M. *Romeo and Juliet.* New York: Spark Publishing, 2008.

## Shakespeare's play name: The <u>Manga Edition</u> Series

Each play in the series is illustrated in the Japanese manga style.

Sexton, A. *Shakespeare's* Hamlet*: The Manga Edition.* Hoboken, NJ: Wiley, 2008.

———. *Shakespeare's* Julius Caesar*: The Manga Edition.* Hoboken, NJ: Wiley, 2008.

———. *Shakespeare's* Macbeth*: The Manga Edition.* Hoboken, NJ: Wiley, 2008.

———. *Shakespeare's* Romeo and Juliet*: The Manga Edition.* Hoboken, NJ: Wiley, 2008.

# *Grades 3–5*

These two books for younger students by Marcia Williams use a graphic, comic book style to retell the plays in a highly illustrated, charming format, with asides from the audience in the margins.

**Williams, M. *Bravo, Mr. William Shakespeare!*** Cambridge, MA: Candlewick Press, 2000.
    Seven of Shakespeare's plays in graphic format for younger students: *As You Like It, Richard III, Antony and Cleopatra, Much Ado about Nothing, Twelfth Night, King Lear,* and *The Merchant of Venice.*

————. *Tales from Shakespeare.* Cambridge, MA: Candlewick Press, 2004.

Seven of Shakespeare's plays in graphic format for younger children: *Romeo and Juliet, A Winter's Tale, Macbeth, A Midsummer Night's Dream, Julius Caesar, Hamlet,* and *The Tempest.*

# Costumes

**Arnold, J.** *Patterns of Fashion: The Cut and Construction of Clothes for Men and Women c. 1560–1620.* Macmillan London Limited, 1985.

A collection of actual patterns for Renaissance clothing, which could be used to make authentic costumes for a play, or simply to read for interest. I bought my copy at the Ashland Oregon Shakespeare Festival bookstore, put it in my Shakespeare library, and found that my students who were performing the plays loved to pore over the pages.

**Hartley, P.** *Medieval Costume and How to Recreate It.* Dover Publications, 2003.

Illustrations and patterns for 200 period costumes of the twelfth to fifteenth centuries.

**Mikhaila, N.** *Tudor Tailor: Reconstructing Sixteenth-century Dress.* Costume & Fashion Press, 2006.

Most useful to students and teachers in this serious costume book is a series of over 40 line drawings, plus photographs, historical portraits, and information on the construction of costumes.

**Norris, H.** *Tudor Costume and Fashion.* Dover Publications, 1997.

Information on and illustrations of an extensive collection of clothing: 1,000 black-and-white figures, 24 half-tones, and 22 color plates.

**Pendergast, S., and T. Pendergast.** <u>Fashion, Costume, and Culture: Clothing, Headwear, Body Decorations, and Footwear through the Ages</u>. UXL, 2004.

*Volume 1.: The Ancient World.*
*Volume 2.: Early Cultures Across the Globe.*
*Volume 3: European Culture from the Renaissance to the Modern Era.*

Volume 1 in this series includes ancient Greek and Roman costume, a source of ideas for Shakespeare's plays with a classical setting such as *Julius Caesar, The Comedy of Errors,* and *A Midsummer Night's Dream.* Volume 2 includes costume of nomads, barbarians, and the Middle Ages, a source of ideas for *Macbeth* and *Richard III.* Note that volumes 1 and 2 show historically accurate partial nudity in some illustrations. Volume 3 includes early to late Renaissance costume, useful for *Hamlet, Romeo and Juliet, The Taming of the Shrew, The Tempest,* and *Twelfth Night.*

**Rowland-Warne, L.** *Costume: An Eyewitness Book.* New York: DK Publishing, 2000.

A richly detailed history of costume covering all periods of Shakespeare's plays, highly illustrated with photographs and drawings.

**Thursfield, S.** *The Medieval Tailor's Assistant.* Costume & Fashion Press, 2001.

An interesting resource showing how common garments were actually made from 1200 to 1500, with 400 line drawings and 121 patterns.

**Tierney, T.** *Renaissance Fashions.* Dover Publications, 2000.

————. *Tudor and Elizabethan Fashion.* Dover Publications, 2000.

These paperback books by Tierney have wonderful color illustrations of costumes of each of these periods.

**Ventura, P.** *Clothing.* New York: Houghton Mifflin, 1992.
> Ideas for Greek, Roman, barbarian, Middle Ages, and Renaissance costuming are shown. Note that some illustrations show historically accurate partial nudity.

## Food and music

**Aliki.** *A Medieval Feast.* New York: HarperCollins, 1986.
> A picture book in Aliki's highly detailed, engaging illustrating style, based on the information we have about feasts during the time of *Macbeth* or *Richard III.*

***The Folger Consort Playing with Fire: The Art of the Instrumentalist.*** Washington, DC: Folger Shakespeare Library, 1995.
> A 61-minute CD of popular tunes of the 1500s and dance music of France and Italy.

**Segan, F., T. Turner, and P. O'Connell.** *Shakespeare's Kitchen.* New York: Random House, 2003.
> A combination of Elizabethan food, culture, and traditional recipes that can be re-created today.

## Warriors and weapons

Weapons play a central role in many of Shakespeare's works, and books that provide factual historical information on them are often fascinating to students performing his plays.

**Boos, B.** *Swords.* Cambridge, MA: Candlewick Press, 2008.
> The author/illustrator describes this absolutely beautiful book as "an artist's devotion." He has drawn and explained swords through the ages, in both real and fantasy worlds. It was an International Reading Association Children's Choices for 2009 starred book, which means it received the highest Children's Choices Team votes.

**Byam, M.** *Arms and Armor: An Eyewitness Book.* New York: DK Publishing, 2002.

**Holmes, R.** *Battle: An Eyewitness Book.* New York: DK Publishing, 2009.
> The highly illustrated and detailed <u>Eyewitness Books</u> should interest many students, and these two include information on the Roman armies of Julius Caesar's time, the medieval warriors of the time of *Macbeth* and *Richard III*, and fighting and warfare during the Renaissance.

# TEACHER RESOURCES

## Books

**Foster, C., and L. G. Johnson.** *Shakespeare: To Teach or Not to Teach: Teaching Shakespeare Made Fun: From Elementary to High School.* Chandler, AZ: Five Star Publications, 2004.
> Information for teachers on Shakespeare and his time, an introduction to the plays for students, and teaching ideas.

**Gibson, R.** *Stepping into Shakespeare.* Cambridge, UK: Cambridge University Press, 2001.
> A handbook of ideas for teaching the language of Shakespeare's plays to address the National Literacy Strategy Range of Reading for Year 6 in Great Britain.

———. *Teaching Shakespeare: A Handbook for Teachers*. Cambridge, UK: Cambridge University Press, 1998.

This is a teaching resource for the elementary through secondary classroom, based on principles of successful teaching about Shakespeare's texts.

**Marland, M.** *Starting Shakespeare*. New York: Pearson/Longman, 1997.

This book includes scenes from several plays, along with classroom activities for discussion, drama, and language study for elementary through middle school.

**Miller, N. J., ed.** *Reimagining Shakespeare for Children and Young Adults*. London: Routledge, 2003.

A collection of essays, including some by several children's authors and illustrators: Aliki, Bruce Coville, Diane Stanley, Marcia Williams, and Gary Blackwood.

**Nelson, P., and T. Daubert.** *Starting with Shakespeare: Successfully Introducing Shakespeare to Children.* Englewood, CO: Teacher Ideas Press/Libraries Unlimited, 2000.

This book provides information and teaching ideas that could supplement teaching Shakespeare through performance: a rationale for using Shakespeare with children; information on Shakespeare's life, works, and language; an introduction to *Hamlet, Macbeth, A Midsummer Night's Dream*, and *Romeo and Juliet*; and samples of students' writing about Shakespeare's plays to illustrate the teaching ideas.

**O'Brien, P., ed.** **Shakespeare Set Free Series,** Vols. I–III. New York: Washington Square Press, 1994, 1995, 2006.

These edited works include in each of the three volumes: essays, step-by-step descriptions of how to help elementary through secondary students approach a text actively, and daily curriculum plans for various plays.

**Reynolds, P.** *Practical Approaches to Teaching Shakespeare*. Cambridge, UK: Cambridge University Press, 2003.

This book offers games, exercises, and music and art ideas for teaching about Shakespeare's plays in the upper elementary classroom.

# Web sites

These Web sites could be useful to teachers and students, but by no means represent a comprehensive list of all Web sites devoted to Shakespeare. Each includes many links to sites that could be relevant to performing Shakespeare's plays with students.

**www.absoluteshakespeare.com**

Summaries and the complete texts of Shakespeare's plays, poems, sonnets, famous quotes, films, trivia, and more are included on this site.

**www.folger.edu/education/teaching.htm**

This Web site of the Folger Shakespeare Library in Washington, D.C., offers resources, teaching ideas, and lesson plans for teaching Shakespeare through performance with children. Of special interest is the Families & Students section, which includes an interactive Web page for students, with samples of Elizabethan music; Shakespeare games; writing challenges; and information about Shakespeare, his plays, and Elizabethan England.

**www.ncte.org**

The Web site of the National Council of Teachers of English includes resources on teaching Shakespeare, as well as lesson plans and teaching ideas submitted by teachers to ReadWriteThink (readwritethink.org), many of which are about Shakespeare for elementary through high school students.

**www.playshakespeare.com**

This Shakespeare resource includes summaries of all the play texts, with an online glossary, reviews, a discussion forum, and links to festivals worldwide.

**www.shakespeares-globe.org**

The official Web site of the reconstructed Globe Theatre in London provides information about the rebuilding of the Globe through the efforts of Sam Wanamaker, an American actor and director. The Globe was first built in 1599 and was where Shakespeare worked and wrote many of his plays until it burned to the ground. The site provides information on current performances and educational events at the Globe, a virtual tour of the Globe, and resources for teachers.

**www.shakespeare.palomar.edu/**

This site is called "Mr. Shakespeare and the Internet," and it endeavors to provide annotated links to every Shakespeare site on the Internet. It also includes time lines, genealogy material, and online versions of important texts.

# Appendix B: *Macbeth* Condensed for Children

### by Carole Cox

## CHARACTERS

Duncan, King of Scotland

Malcolm, his son

Donalbain, his son

Macbeth, a general of the king's army

Banquo, a general of the king's army

Macduff

Lennox, nobleman

Ross, nobleman

Angus, nobleman

Fleance, son of Banquo

A Doctor

A Porter

Lady Macbeth

Gentlewoman, attending Lady Macbeth

Three Witches

Messenger

Soldiers, in battle

From *Shakespeare Kids: Performing his Plays, Speaking his Words* by Carole Cox. Santa Barbara, CA: Libraries Unlimited.
Copyright © 2010. May be copied for classroom use.

# Scene 1: Night on a Battlefield

[*Thunder and lightning. Enter three witches.*]

**First Witch:** When shall we three meet again?

In thunder, lightning, or in rain?

**Second Witch:** When the hurly-burly's done,

When the battle's lost and won.

**Third Witch:** That will be ere the set of sun.

**First Witch:** Where the place?

**Second Witch:** Upon the heath.

**Third Witch:** There to meet with Macbeth.

**All Three:** Fair is foul, and foul is fair;

Hover through the fog and filthy air.

[*Scene of battle. A drum within.*]

**First Witch:** A drum!

**Second Witch:** A drum!

**Third Witch:** Macbeth doth come!

**All Three:** The weird sisters, hand in hand,

Posters of the sea and land,

Thus do go about, about,

Thrice to thine, and thrice to mine,

And thrice again, to make up nine.

Peace! The charm's wound up.

[*Enter Macbeth and Banquo.*]

**Macbeth:** So foul and fair a day I have not seen.

**Banquo:** What are these, so withered and so wild in their attire?

**Macbeth:** Speak, if you can, what are you?

**First Witch:** All hail, Macbeth, hail to thee, Thane of Glamis!

**Second Witch:** All hail, Macbeth, hail to thee, Thane of Cawdor!

**Third Witch:** All hail, Macbeth, hail to thee, that shalt be King hereafter!

**First Witch:** Hail!

**Second Witch:** Hail!

| | |
|---|---|
| **Third Witch:** | Hail! |
| **First Witch:** | Lesser than Macbeth, and greater. |
| **Second Witch:** | Not so happy, yet much happier. |
| **Third Witch:** | Thou shalt get kings, though thou be none. |
| | So all hail, Macbeth and Banquo! |
| **All Three:** | Banquo and Macbeth, all hail! |
| **Macbeth:** | Stay, you imperfect speakers, tell me more: |
| | I know I am Thane of Glamis, |
| | But how of Cawdor? |
| | The Thane of Cawdor lives, |
| | A prosperous gentleman and to be King |
| | Stands not within the prospect of belief, |
| | No more than to be Cawdor. |
| | Say from whence you owe this strange intelligence. |
| | Speak, I charge you! |
| | [*Witches vanish.*] |
| **Banquo:** | The earth hath bubbles as the water has, and these are of them. |
| | Whither are they vanished? |
| **Macbeth:** | Into the air, and what seemed corporal, |
| | Melted, as breath into the wind. |
| | Would they had stayed. |
| **Banquo:** | Were such things here as we do speak about? |
| | Or have we eaten that insane root |
| | That takes the reason prisoner? |
| **Macbeth:** | Your children shall be kings. |
| **Banquo:** | You shall be King. |
| **Macbeth:** | And Thane of Cawdor too they said. |
| | [*Enter Ross and Angus.*] |
| **Ross:** | The King hath happily received, Macbeth, |
| | The news of thy success. |
| **Angus:** | And we are sent to give thee from our royal master thanks. |

**Ross:** And for a greater honor, he bade me call thee Thane of Cawdor.

**Banquo:** What, can the devil speak true?

**Macbeth:** The Thane of Cawdor lives.

**Angus:** Who was the Thane lives yet, but under the heavy judgment of treason is about to lose his life.

**Macbeth:** [*Aside*] Glamis, and now Thane of Cawdor.

If chance will have me king, why, chance may crown me.

**Banquo:** Worthy Macbeth, we stay upon your leisure.

**Macbeth:** Let us toward the King.

[*Exit Banquo, Ross, and Angus.*]

**Macbeth:** Stars, hide your fires,

Let no light see my black and deep desires.

## Scene II: Macbeth's Castle

[*Enter Lady Macbeth, reading a letter.*]

**Lady Macbeth:** Glamis thou art, and Cawdor and shalt be what thou art promised.

Yet I fear thy nature. It is too full of the milk of human kindness.

[*Enter Macbeth.*]

**Lady Macbeth:** Great Glamis, worthy Cawdor, greater than both,

By the all-hail hereafter.

**Macbeth:** My dearest love, Duncan comes here tonight.

**Lady Macbeth:** And when goes hence?

**Macbeth:** Tomorrow.

**Lady Macbeth:** O never shall sun that morrow see.

Bear welcome in your eye, your hand, your tongue;

Look like the innocent flower, but be the serpent under it.

He that's coming must be provided for:

And you shall put this night's great business into my dispatch.

Leave all the rest to me.

[*Exit Macbeth. Music. Enter the King, Malcolm, Donalbain, Banquo, Lennox, Macduff, Ross, Angus, and Attendants.*]

**King Duncan:** See, our honored hostess. We thank you for your trouble.

**Lady Macbeth:** Your majesty fills our house.

**King Duncan:** Give me your hand; conduct me to my host; we love him highly.

[*All exit. Night falls. Torches are lighted. Music is heard. Servants pass.*]

[*Enter Macbeth.*]

**Macbeth:** If it were done when 'tis done, then 'twere well it were done quickly.

That but this assassination might be the be-all and the end-all.

Duncan's here in double trust:

First, as I am his kinsman and his subject, then as his host who should against his murderer shut the door, not bear the knife myself.

[*Enter Lady Macbeth.*]

**Macbeth:** How now? What news?

**Lady Macbeth:** He has almost dined. Why have you left the chamber?

**Macbeth:** We will proceed no further in this murderous business; he hath honored me of late.

**Lady Macbeth:** But where is your desire to be king?

**Macbeth:** I pray thee, peace. I dare do all that may become a man; who dares do more is none.

**Lady Macbeth:** What beast was it then that made you break this enterprise to me?

When you dared do it then you were a man.

**Macbeth:** If we should fail—

**Lady Macbeth:** We fail? But screw your courage to the sticking-place and we'll not fail.

When Duncan is asleep, we'll drug his servants.

What cannot you and I perform upon the unguarded Duncan.

**Macbeth:** We'll use the servants daggers and mark them with his blood.

Who'll not believe they've done it?

**Lady Macbeth:** Who'll dare not believe it?

**Macbeth:** I am settled to this terrible feat.

False face must hide what the false heart doth know.

[*Exit.*]

[*Enter Banquo; Fleance, his son; and a torchbearer.*]

**Banquo:** How goes the night my son?

**Fleance:** The moon is down; I have not heard the clock.

**Banquo:** And she goes down at midnight.

**Fleance:** I take it, 'tis later, sir.

**Banquo:** A heavy summons lies like lead upon me. And yet I would not sleep.

*[Enter Macbeth and a Servant with a torch.]*

**Banquo:** Who's there?

**Macbeth:** A friend.

**Banquo:** What, sir, not yet at rest? The King's in bed. I dreamt last night of the three weird sisters. To you they have showed some truth.

**Macbeth:** I think not of them. Good repose to you.

**Banquo:** Thanks sir; the like to you.

*[Exit Banquo and Fleance.]*

**Macbeth:** Go bid thy mistress, when my drink is ready; to strike upon the bell. Get thee to bed.

*[Exit Servant.]*

**Macbeth:** Is this a dagger which I see before me, the handle toward my hand?

Come, let me clutch thee.

I have thee not, and yet I see thee still;

and on thy blade and handle gouts of blood.

*[A bell rings.]*

**Macbeth:** I go, and it is done; the bell invites me.

Hear it not, Duncan, for it is your death knell that summons thee to heaven or to hell.

*[Exit Macbeth.]*

*[Enter Lady Macbeth.]*

**Lady Macbeth:** Hark, I laid their daggers ready. He could not miss 'em.

Had he not resembled my father as he slept I would have killed him myself.

*[Enter Macbeth.]*

**Macbeth:** I have done the deed. Didst thou not hear a noise?

**Lady Macbeth:** I heard the owl scream and the crickets cry.

**Macbeth:** Me thought I heard a voice cry, "Sleep no more; Macbeth does murder sleep"—

the innocent sleep,

"Macbeth shall sleep no more."

**Lady Macbeth:** You do unbend your noble strength to think so brainsickly of things.

Go get some water and wash this filthy witness from your hand.

Why did you bring the daggers? They must be found there. Go carry them and smear the sleepy servants with blood.

**Macbeth:** I'll go no more. I am afraid to think what I have done; look on it again I dare not.

**Lady Macbeth:** Infirm of purpose;

Give me the daggers.

If he bleeds I'll smear the faces of the servants, for it must seem their guilt.

[*Exit Lady Macbeth. A knock.*]

**Macbeth:** Whence is that knocking? How is it with me, when every noise appalls me?

Will all great Neptune's ocean wash this blood clean from my hand?

[*Enter Lady Macbeth,*]

**Lady Macbeth:** My hands are of your color, but I shame to wear a heart so white.

[*Knock.*]

**Lady Macbeth:** I hear a knocking. We'll go to our room. A little water clears us of this deed. How easy it is then.

[*Knock.*]

**Lady Macbeth:** Hark! More knocking.

[*Knock.*]

**Macbeth:** Wake Duncan with your knocking. I wish thou could.

[*Exit.*]

[*Enter a Porter. More knocking.*]

**Porter:** Knock! Knock! Knock! Who's there in the name of Beelzebub?

[*Opens the gate.*]

[*Enter Macduff and Lennox.*]

**Macduff:** Is thy master stirring?

[*Enter Macbeth.*]

**Macduff:** Our knocking has awakened him; here he comes.

**Lennox:** Good morrow, noble sir.

**Macbeth:** Good morrow noble Macduff, Lennox.

**Macduff:** Is the King stirring, worthy thane?

**Macbeth:** Not yet. I'll bring you to him. This is the door.

**Macduff:** I'll make so bold to call.

[*Exit Macduff.*]

**Lennox:** Does the king leave today?

**Macbeth:** He did say so.

**Lennox:** The night has been unruly. Where we lay, our chimneys were blown down, and as they say, lamentings heard in the air, strange screams of death and prophesying of confused events. Some say the earth was feverous and did shake.

**Macbeth:** 'Twas a rough night.

[*Enter Macduff.*]

**Macduff:** O horror, horror, horror!

**Lennox:** What's the matter?

**Macduff:** Most sacrilegious murder hath been done.

**Macbeth:** What is it you say?

**Lennox:** Mean you his majesty?

**Macduff:** Do not bid me speak. See, and speak yourselves.

[*Exit Macbeth and Lennox.*]

**Macduff:** Awake! Awake! Ring the alarm-bell. Murder and treason.

[*Bell rings.*]

**Lady Macbeth:** What's the business? Speak!

**Macduff:** O gentle lady, 'tis not for you to hear what I can speak.

[*Enter Banquo.*]

**Macduff:** O Banquo, Banquo, our royal master's murdered.

**Lady Macbeth:** What, in our house?

**Banquo:** Too cruel anywhere. Say it is not so.

[*Enter Malcolm, Donalbain, and others,*]

118

**Donalbain:** What is amiss?

**Macduff:** Your royal father's murdered.

**Malcolm:** O, by whom?

**Lennox:** His servants it seems. Their hands and faces were covered with blood; So were their daggers we found upon their pillows.

**Lady Macbeth:** Help me hence!

**Macduff:** Look to the lady.

**Malcolm:** [*Aside to Donalbain.*] Why do we hold our tongues?

**Donalbain:** [*Aside to Malcolm.*] What should be spoken here, where our fate may rush and seize us?

**Macduff:** Look to the lady, Ho;

We will question this most bloody piece of work to know it further.

[*All exit except Malcolm and Donalbain.*]

[*Lady Macbeth is carried out.*]

**Malcolm:** Let's not consort with them. I'll to England.

**Donalbain:** To Ireland I; our separation shall keep us both safer. Where we are there's daggers in men's smiles.

**Malcolm:** Therefore to horse; and let us not be dainty of leave-taking.

# Scene III: The Heath

[*Thunder. Enter the three Witches.*]

**First Witch:** Thrice the brinded cat hath mewed.

**Second Witch:** Thrice, and once the hedge-pig whined.

**Third Witch:** Harpier cries; 'tis time; 'tis time.

**First Witch:** Round about the cauldron go; in the poisoned entrails throw.

**All Three:** Double, double, toil and trouble;

Fire burn, and cauldron bubble.

**Third Witch:** Scale of dragon, tooth of wolf, witches' mummy, maw and gulf of the ravened salt-sea shark; root of hemlock, digged in the dark.

**All Three:** Double, double, toil, and trouble; fire burn and cauldron bubble.

**First Witch:** Cool it with a baboon's blood, then the charm is firm and good.

**Second Witch:** By the pricking of my thumbs, something wicked this way comes.

Open, locks, whoever knocks.

[*Enter Macbeth.*]

**Macbeth:** How now, you secret, black, and midnight hags? What is it you do?

**All Three:** A deed without a name. We know thy thought:

hear our speech, but say thou nought.

**First Witch:** Macbeth! Macbeth! Macbeth! Beware Macduff.

**Second Witch:** Macbeth! Macbeth! Macbeth! Be bloody bold and resolute; laugh to scorn the power of man; for none of woman born shall harm Macbeth.

**Macbeth:** Then live Macduff; what need I fear of thee? But yet . . . I'll make double sure. Thou shalt not live.

**Third Witch:** Macbeth shall never be vanquished until great Birnam Wood comes to high Dunsinane Hill.

**Macbeth:** That will never be. Who can make the forest, or tell the tree to move his root?

[*Witches vanish.*]

**Macbeth:** Where are they? Gone? Come in you there!

[*Enter Lennox.*]

**Lennox:** What's your Grace's will?

**Macbeth:** Saw you the weird sisters?

**Lennox:** No, my lord.

**Macbeth:** Came they not by you!

**Lennox:** No indeed, my lord.

**Macbeth:** Infected be the air whereon they ride, and damned all those that trust them. I did hear the galloping of a horse; who was it came by?

**Lennox:** Macduff is fled to England.

**Macbeth:** Fled to England?

**Lennox:** Aye, my good lord.

**Macbeth:** So, the castle of Macduff I will surprise, seize his lands, give to the edge of the sword his wife, his babes, and all unfortunate souls who belong to his family. No boasting like a fool; this deed I'll do before the purpose cool.

# Scene IV: England

*[Enter Malcolm and Macduff.]*

**Macduff:** O Scotland, Scotland! With an untitled tyrant bloody-sceptered, when shalt thou see thy wholesome days again?

**Malcolm:** I think our country sinks beneath the yoke; it weeps, it bleeds.

*[Enter Ross.]*

**Macduff:** See who comes here.

**Malcolm:** It is my countryman.

**Macduff:** My ever gentle cousin, welcome hither. Stands Scotland where it did?

**Ross:** Alas poor country, almost afraid to know itself. It cannot be called our mother, but our grave.

**Macduff:** What's the newest grief?

**Ross:** Let not your ears despise my tongue forever. Your castle is surprised; your wife and babes savagely slaughtered. To relate the manner would add the death of you.

**Macduff:** My children too? My wife killed too?

**Ross:** I have said.

**Macduff:** All my pretty ones? Did you say all? O hell-kite! All? At one fell swoop?

**Malcolm:** Dispute it like a man.

**Macduff:** I shall do so. But I must also feel it as a man. Did heaven look on and would not take their part?

**Malcolm:** Be this the whetstone of your sword; let grief convert to anger.

**Macduff:** Front to front bring thou this fiend of Scotland and myself;

within my sword's length set him;

if he escape, heaven forgive him too.

**Malcolm:** This tune goes manly. Come, we go to the King; our power is ready. Macbeth is ripe for shaking. Receive what cheer you may; the night is long that never finds the day.

# Scene V: Dunsinane Castle

[*Enter a Doctor and a waiting Gentlewoman.*]

**Doctor:** I have two nights watched with you, but can perceive no truth in your report. When was it she last walked?

**Gentlewoman:** Lo you, here she comes.

[*Enter Lady Macbeth.*]

**Gentlewoman:** She is fast asleep. Observe her; stand close.

**Doctor:** You see her eyes are open.

**Gentlewoman:** Ay, but their sense is shut.

**Doctor:** What is it she does now? Look how she rubs her hands.

**Gentlewoman:** It is an accustomed action with her, to seem thus washing her hands. I have seen her do it a quarter of an hour.

**Lady Macbeth:** Yet here's a spot.

Out damned spot! Out, I say!

One; two. Why, then 'tis time to do it. Hell is murky.

Fie, my lord, fie! A soldier and afraid?

Yet who would have thought the old man to have so much blood in him?

**Doctor:** Do you mark that?

**Lady Macbeth:** Macduff, the Thane of Fife had a wife. Where is she now? What, will these hands never be clean? Here's the smell of the blood still. All the perfumes of Arabia will not sweeten this little hand. Oh, oh, oh!

**Doctor:** What a sigh is there! The heart is sorely charged.

**Gentlewoman:** I would not have such a heart in my bosom.

**Lady Macbeth:** Wash your hands, look not so pale.

I tell you again, Banquo's buried;

he cannot come out on his grave.

**Doctor:** Even so?

**Lady Macbeth:** Tomorrow, and tomorrow, and tomorrow,

Creeps in this petty pace from day to day,

to the last syllable of recorded time:

and all our yesterdays have lighted fools the way to dusty death.

Out, out, brief candle. Life's but a walking shadow,

a poor player that struts and frets his hour upon the stage,

and then is heard no more.

It is a tale told by an idiot, full of sound and fury,

signifying nothing.

[*She pauses and then looks up as if she hears a noise.*]

**Lady Macbeth:** To bed, to bed:

there's knocking at the gate.

Come, come, come, come, give me your hand.

What's done cannot be undone.

To bed, to bed, to bed.

**Doctor:** Will she go now to bed?

**Gentlewoman:** Directly.

**Doctor:** God, God forgive us all. Look after her;

I think but dare not speak.

**Gentlewoman:** Good night, good doctor.

# Scene VI: Dunsinane

[*Enter Macbeth, then Messenger.*]

**Messenger:** Gracious milord, I should report that which I say I saw, but know not how to do it.

**Macbeth:** Well say sir.

**Messenger:** As I did stand my watch upon the hill I looked toward Birnam Wood and anon, me thought the wood began to move.

**Macbeth:** Liar and slave.

**Messenger:** Let me endure your wrath if it be not so;

within this three mile may you see it coming;

I say, a moving forest.

**Macbeth:** If thou speakest false, upon the next tree shalt thou hang alive.

I doubt the prophesy of the witches that lie like truth.

"Fear not til Birnam Wood do come to Dunsinane,"

and now a wood comes toward Dunsinane.

Arm, arm, and out,

Ring the alarm bell!

Blow, wind! Come wrack!

At least we'll die with harness on our back.

[*Malcolm and his army storm the castle. Drum and colors. Men enter with their boughs. Alarm bell, trumpets, swords, men run. Enter Macduff.*]

**Macduff:** Tyrant show they face! Turn, hell-hound, turn.

**Macbeth:** Of all men else I have avoided thee.

But get thee back, my soul is too much charged with blood of thine already.

**Macduff:** I have no words;

my voice is in my sword, thou bloodier villain than terms can give thee out!

[*They fight.*]

**Macbeth:** Thou losest labor. I bear a charmed life, which must not yield to one of woman born.

**Macduff:** Despair thy charm;

Macduff was from his mother's womb untimely ripped.

**Macbeth:** I'll not fight with thee.

**Macduff:** Then yield thee coward.

**Macbeth:** I will not yield. Lay on Macduff, and damned be him that first cries, "Hold, enough!"

[*Macduff kills Macbeth. Malcolm and others enter. Drum and colors. Soldiers.*]

**Macduff:** Hail King! For so thou art.

Behold where lies the tyrants cursed head:

The time is free. Hail king of Scotland!

**Soldiers and All:** Hail, King of Scotland.

# Index

# About the Author

Photo by Brenda Teepell

Carole Cox has been a professor at Louisiana State University, Baton Rouge, and is now at California State University, Long Beach, where she teaches language arts and literacy education classes. She taught elementary school in Los Angeles, California, and Madison, Wisconsin. She is the author of many articles and books in education, most recently *Teaching Language Arts: A Student-centered Classroom* (2008) and *Engaging English Learners: Exploring Literature, Developing Literacy, and Differentiating Instruction*, coauthored with Paul Boyd-Batstone (2009). In 2001 she was named the Outstanding Professor at California State University, Long Beach. Her former elementary students from 1967 to 1970, whom you will read about in this book, arranged for Mayor David J. Cieslewicz to issue a mayoral proclamation declaring July 2, 2005, Carole Cox Day in Madison during a reunion they planned for her former students and participants in the "Shakespeare for Kids" summer program she created in Madison in 1971.

Franklin Pierce University

00186675